TOM'S
TABLE

TOM'S TABLE

MY FAVOURITE EVERYDAY RECIPES

TOM KERRIDGE

Thanks once again to my amazing wife Bef for

putting up with the late nights, early mornings

and broken sleep. You really are the most

important thing in the world!

Big love, Tom x

Running a restaurant and a pub is a lot of hard work, so it's a good job I love it! Serving up great meals to happy customers is just about the best way of earning a living I can think of, and although the hours are long and sometimes it's stressful trying to get everything right, I wouldn't have it any other way.

When I get home after a long day's work, I always plan to put my feet up. But before I know it I'm going through the fridge instead: chopping and stirring, seasoning and tasting, and coming up with new ideas. It's play to me – relaxing and exciting at the same time, even when I'm tired. Using what I've got to hand to create something delicious, without the pressure of a room full of diners waiting to be served... I can lose hours that way.

At home, I still go for the same big, bold and complex flavours I strive for at work. I figure there are only so many meals you are going to get to eat in your life, so they might as well all be as brilliant as you can make them! Don't get me wrong, I'm as likely to have a slice of toast or a bacon sarnie on the hoof as anyone, but when I have a bit more time, I like to make every meal as special as I can.

These recipes are favourites from my own kitchen, the ones I really enjoy with my wife Beth and our friends, whether it's a nice dinner round the table or a summer barbecue in the garden. When I'm at home, I might pare down some of the techniques our customers expect from our two-Michelin-starred restaurant, but I don't pare down the taste. I still go for my preferred flavours and textures, often with a bit of surprise and dazzle thrown in.

As you'll know, I love British food and I've included some of my tried-and-trusted favourites here, such as cosy Cheddar and ale soup and tasty weekend roast chicken, but I've cast my net beyond our shores and pulled in some great dishes from the rest of Europe, America and the Caribbean too. So crab cakes sit alongside clam chowder, roast rump of lamb alongside jerk chicken, and carrot cake alongside popcorn bars. It's really comfort food at its best.

While some of the recipes might not be exactly familiar, they can all sit quite comfortably on the British table – after all, we're among the most adventurous eaters on the planet! While we love fish and chips, bangers and mash, and toad in-the-hole, we'll also happily tuck into

a great curry or pizza, and we will chuck a shish kebab on the grill as eagerly as we will a juicy steak. We don't stand too much on ceremony – if it tastes good, we want to eat it.

I've avoided cheffy techniques in these recipes, so nothing's too complicated. Some of the dishes might require a bit of time – letting foods develop complex flavours with rubs or marinades, or become really tender with slow simmering – but you don't have to do anything much more taxing than wait while they get on with it. Even if you haven't done much cooking before, I'd encourage you just to get stuck in and have a go. If it's not absolutely perfect, who cares? It's still going to be really tasty.

Lots of the recipes can be made well ahead – some as much as a day or two before you want to eat them – and just reheated. So if you're throwing a party, you can spare yourself the last-minute stress, or if you have a busy week ahead, take some time at the weekend to prepare something like a venison chilli or meatballs in treacle gravy so you have a few easy dinners on hand during the week. Most of the recipes here aren't rushed; in fact very few need to be served the minute they're done.

I've included some of my favourite ways to whack in lots of flavour. I never miss a chance to give a dish extra depth and interest; I taste all of the time and tweak the seasoning as I go. It's no good just tossing in a load of salt and pepper right at the end – you want the seasoning to be layered all the way through the dish, to get a good balance and make everything taste as good as it possibly can.

I'm giving you other great tips too, such as how to brown meat properly, especially minced meat for things like my green chilli con carne. You want to get it good and brown, taking it almost as far as you dare, until it's virtually coffee-granule brown and really crispy, because that's where the flavour comes from. Once you've tried this in one of my recipes, I hope you'll take that technique and use it whenever you cook a meat sauce. It's a simple thing which transforms a straightforward dish into something really special, and that's what I try to do with every dish, every day, whether I'm at work or at home.

By popular demand, I've included a lot more sweet things in this book, from classics like crème caramel, baked cheesecake and blueberry muffins, to more adventurous whisky and rye puddings, blitz torte and peanut butter, black cherry and chocolate tart. But of course, I couldn't resist giving these sweets my own twists. So expect a hit of chilli in the rocky road and a slug of rum in the date and banana milk shake... you have been warned.

My dishes are not about showing off. They're about pleasure and generosity. They're about sitting around a table with people you like and sharing a drink, something good to eat, a great conversation and a few laughs. And the food can be something as simple as a couple of pork burgers and salad on a Tuesday night after work, or a big Saturday night blow out with a crowd. The key thing is to have fun too, in the kitchen and at the table, so don't be a martyr.

If you don't have the time, or you just don't fancy it, there's no need to make every item from scratch. Concentrate on one or two great dishes, and serve them with a crisp green salad or some simply boiled potatoes or steamed rice. Of course, if you have got time, knock yourself out and make everything from bread to pud – the important thing is that you enjoy yourself, because somehow that always makes everything taste better!

SNACKS & STARTERS

In this chapter, I'd really be letting my hair down, if I had any! I love thinking up great starters and small dishes, because they are an opportunity to set out your stall, to let people know they're in for a good time. You can be quite adventurous and experiment with techniques, flavours and textures. And you can have a bit of fun too, which is why I've included some of my favourite snacks such as the cheesy tostadas and corn dogs – you can't take life too seriously when you're eating a corn dog!

Sometimes you really want to perk up your tastebuds, whether it's at the beginning of a meal or with a quick snack, and this is when I ramp up the chillies. I love to add a bit of fire when I can, so to a tasty grilled cheese and ham sandwich I add chopped pickled green chillies. They lend heat and acidity, in the same way as a smear of English mustard or some good chutney might. And you can't beat buffalo chicken wings for a lively, mouth-tingling blast of heat... But there's room for more subtle dishes too, such as blue cheese tart, matzo ball soup or knish – those cosy little potato buns that are so great either on their own or with a good bowl of soup.

And, of course, you can tweak most of the dishes here a bit and turn them into fantastic main courses. It could be as simple as making a salad of bitter leaves to go with the blue cheese tart or ladling an extra scoop of the matzo ball soup into the bowl. Or with the borscht, you might want to spoon on some shredded duck and a glistening spoonful of avruga caviar to give it the full-on glam treatment. Who wouldn't love that?

CRISPY CHEESY TOSTADAS

I love these Mexican-inspired snacks. They have the perfect balance of texture, spice and savoury flavour. Stack them up like a pile of poppadoms, stick them in the middle of the table and let everyone get stuck in. This is a great recipe for a late-night crowd, as you can easily double or even triple it up. MAKES 8

500g minced pork
8 ripe plum tomatoes
2 tsp cumin seeds
2 tsp coriander seeds
½ tsp smoked paprika
½ tsp cracked black pepper
3 green chillies, diced (seeds and all)
4 pickled green chillies, sliced
8 flour tortillas
250g strong Cheddar cheese, grated
Salt

Heat a large, non-stick frying pan over a medium heat. Add the minced pork and dry-fry for about 20–25 minutes, stirring frequently, until the mince is nicely browned – it should have a crisp and crunchy texture. Drain the mince in a colander to remove any excess fat. Wipe out the pan with kitchen paper.

While the mince is cooking, prepare the tomatoes. Have a bowl of iced water ready and bring a saucepan of water to the boil. Immerse the tomatoes in the boiling water for 10–15 seconds then immediately plunge into the iced water to stop them cooking. Peel, quarter, deseed and dice the tomatoes; set aside.

Preheat the oven to 160°C/Fan 140°C/Gas 3.

Return the frying pan to a medium heat. Add the cumin and coriander seeds and toast for a couple of minutes, rattling the pan, until they're fragrant – be careful not to burn them. Remove from the pan and cool slightly. Using an electric spice grinder or pestle and mortar, grind the seeds to a fine powder.

Return the ground spices to the pan, along with the smoked paprika and black pepper, and heat gently for 1 minute. Stir in the mince and chopped fresh chillies. Heat for a further couple of minutes, then season well with salt. Stir in the pickled chillies and diced tomatoes and cook very gently, stirring from time to time, for about 10 minutes until the sauce is thickened.

Meanwhile, lay the tortillas on 2 or 3 baking sheets and bake for 8–10 minutes until lightly browned. Remove from the oven and whack the oven temperature up to 220°C/Fan 200°C/Gas 7.

Spread the pork mixture evenly over the tortillas and scatter the grated cheese on top. Return to the oven for 5 minutes until the cheese is melted and bubbling and the tortillas are crisp. Stack them on a large plate and serve.

CHEESE, HAM &
PICKLED CHILLI TOASTIE

This is my super-deluxe version of cheese on toast. I use pickled green chillies, but gherkins, capers or even pickled onions would work too – they give a lovely, sharp acidity to the sandwich. The Parmesan crisp is an added delicious bonus, but it's not essential – simply omit it for a quick toastie. MAKES 1

30g butter, softened
2 slices of sandwich bread
100g cheese (ideally Comté, Gruyère or Emmental, but a strong Cheddar is good too), sliced
1 thick slice of good smoked ham
1 tbsp chopped pickled green chillies

For the Parmesan crisp
15–20g Parmesan cheese, freshly grated

Preheat the oven to 180°C/Fan 160°C/Gas 4.

Heat a large, non-stick frying pan over a medium heat. Spread the butter on one side of the bread slices.

Place one bread slice, butter side down, in the pan. Now assemble the sandwich directly in the pan. Lay half of the cheese slices on top of the bread, followed by the ham. Scatter on the chopped chillies and place the remaining sliced cheese on top. Cover with the other bread slice, butter side up, and press gently to squeeze everything together.

Cook the sandwich for a few minutes until the bottom is lovely and golden brown. Carefully flip over and cook the other side for a further few minutes until browned and the cheese is oozing and melted, about 3 minutes each side should do it.

Transfer the toasted sandwich to a baking tray and place in the oven for 5 minutes to ensure the cheese melts completely.

Meanwhile, for the Parmesan crisp, wipe the pan clean with kitchen paper and place over a medium-low heat. Sprinkle the Parmesan in an even layer in the centre of the pan. Cook gently for 3–4 minutes until the Parmesan has melted and is nicely golden brown and crisp.

Quickly remove the Parmesan crisp from the pan and, while it's still warm, pop it inside or on top of the grilled cheese sandwich. Serve straight away.

BEEF FLANK JERKY

This jerky makes a great, meaty, tasty snack – it's packed full of savoury umami flavour and is incredibly moreish. It's particularly good with a cold glass of beer. Jerky is normally air-dried, but I bake these steak strips and then store them in an airtight container in the fridge, where they'll keep quite well for a couple of weeks. You can halve the amount of beef used here if you like, but keep the marinade quantities the same. MAKES ABOUT 650g

1kg beef flank steak, in one piece
100ml dark soy sauce
3 garlic cloves, finely grated
3 tsp cracked black pepper
1 tsp ground allspice
½ tsp salt
2 tsp smoked paprika

Place the beef, well wrapped, in the freezer for 30 minutes or so – this makes it a lot easier to slice.

Using a sharp knife, slice the steak lengthways, as thinly as you can, going with the grain of the meat. Set aside.

In a large bowl, mix together the soy sauce, garlic, pepper, allspice and salt. Add the beef to the bowl and toss together to coat the strips evenly in the mixture. Cover the bowl with cling film and place in the fridge. Leave to marinate for at least 3 hours or longer if you can, preferably overnight.

Remove the beef from the fridge around 30 minutes before you are going to cook it, to let it come to room temperature.

Preheat the oven to 120°C/Fan 100°C/Gas ½.

Sit a wire cooling rack over the top of a baking tray or roasting tin. Remove the beef strips from the marinade and arrange on the wire rack – you may need to use 2 trays and wire racks, depending on their size.

Sprinkle the smoked paprika evenly over the beef. Bake for 3–4 hours, until it's crispy, dark brown, dry and brittle. Once cooked, remove from the oven and allow the jerky to cool before serving.

Serve as a snack, or store in an airtight container in the fridge until ready to eat.

KNISH

These great little potato buns have been a popular East European street food for centuries and they are loved all around the world. Mine are filled with potato and matzo meal, so they're quite carb heavy, but they go so well with soups or vegetable stews, or you can just eat them on their own as a snack. Once you've mastered the method, you can customise the filling and make them your own with minced meats, sauerkraut, cheese, herbs, almost whatever takes your fancy. MAKES 7

For the potato filling

300g floury potatoes, such as Maris Piper or King Edward, peeled and cut into 4cm dice

2 tbsp vegetable oil

1 large onion, finely diced

2 garlic cloves, finely grated

3 tbsp matzo meal or dry breadcrumbs

2 tsp caster sugar

1 egg, beaten

Salt and freshly ground black pepper

For the dough

200g plain flour, plus extra for dusting

1 tsp baking powder

½ tsp salt

2 tbsp vegetable oil, plus extra for greasing

1 egg

3 tbsp cold water

For the eggwash

2 egg yolks, mixed with a splash of milk

To make the potato filling, bring a medium saucepan of salted water to the boil. Add the diced potatoes and cook for around 10-12 minutes until tender. Drain in a colander and leave for a few minutes to allow the potatoes to steam and dry out.

Meanwhile, heat a frying pan over a medium heat and add the oil. When it is hot, add the onion and garlic and sweat for around 10-12 minutes until soft and deep golden - you want the onion to be quite caramelised.

Transfer the onion and garlic to a large bowl, add the potatoes and mash together well until smooth. Stir in the matzo meal, sugar and beaten egg. Season generously with salt and pepper and mix well to combine. Cover with cling film and place in the fridge to chill.

To make the dough, put the flour, baking powder, salt, oil, egg and water in a freestanding electric mixer fitted with the dough hook (or into a food processor), and mix to a soft, pliable dough. Wrap the dough in cling film and chill in the fridge for an hour.

Preheat the oven to 180°C/Fan 160°C/Gas 4. Lightly grease a large baking tray.

Using a lightly floured rolling pin, roll the dough out as thinly as possible on a floured surface to a 30cm square.

Spoon the potato filling into the centre of the dough and spread it out evenly, leaving a 2-3cm clear margin. Brush the edges of the dough with egg wash, then roll up tightly like a Swiss roll. Press the ends together with your fingers to seal.

Divide the roll of filled dough into 7 portions, by pressing down with the side of your hand at 6 evenly spaced intervals. Using a knife, cut where you've pressed down, to separate the buns.

Gently press and pinch the open edges together to seal the buns, shaping them gently with your hands.

Place the buns flat side down on the prepared baking tray and brush each one generously with egg wash. Bake for 40–50 minutes, until golden brown and crisp.

Serve the knish warm, on their own as a snack, or floating in bowls of soup or stew.

RUNZAS

I think of runzas as a far-flung cousin of our much-loved Cornish pasties. They originated in nineteenth-century Russia then travelled to Germany and the Americas. Fitting conveniently into a pocket, runzas were often taken to the fields by farmers to savour as a working lunch. With a minced beef and cabbage filling, encased in a yeasted dough, they have a slight 'chew' to them, which I really like. MAKES 12

For the dough
650g strong white bread
    flour, plus extra for
    dusting
60g caster sugar
1 tsp salt
1 tsp fast-action dried yeast
320ml warm milk
75g butter, melted and
    cooled slightly
2 eggs
A little vegetable oil, for
    oiling the bowl

For the beef filling
600g minced beef
3 tbsp vegetable oil
2 onions, finely chopped
½ spring cabbage (about
    250g), finely shredded
4 tbsp Dijon mustard
2 tbsp Bovril
2 tbsp caraway seeds
Salt and freshly ground
    black pepper

For the glaze
50g butter, melted and
    cooled

To make the dough, put the flour, sugar, salt and yeast into a freestanding electric mixer fitted with the paddle attachment and mix to combine. In a small bowl, whisk together the warm milk, melted butter and eggs. Pour this liquid into the mixer and mix to form a dough. Knead in the mixer for 8–10 minutes, on a medium setting, until soft, smooth and elastic.

Transfer the dough to a clean, lightly oiled bowl and cover with a damp tea towel. Leave to rise in a warm place for 30–40 minutes until it is soft and slightly aerated.

Lift the risen dough out of the bowl and place on a lightly floured surface. Knock it back, then knead with your hands for 5–10 minutes. Return to the bowl, cover and leave to prove for 30–40 minutes.

Meanwhile, make the filling. Heat a large, non-stick frying pan over a medium heat. Add the minced beef and dry-fry for about 20–25 minutes, stirring frequently, until it is nicely browned – it should have a crisp and crunchy texture.

Drain the crispy beef in a colander to remove any excess fat, then tip into a large bowl; set aside.

Heat 2 tbsp of the oil in the frying pan. Add the onions and cook over a medium-low heat for around 10 minutes until softened. Transfer the onions to the bowl with the beef.

Crank up the heat under the pan and add the remaining 1 tbsp oil. Tip the shredded cabbage into the pan and wilt quickly for a few minutes, stirring frequently. Add the cabbage to the beef and onions, then stir in the mustard, Bovril and caraway seeds. Season generously with salt and pepper.

After proving, knock back the dough on a lightly floured surface and divide into 12 equal-sized pieces, shaping them into balls with your hands. Using a lightly floured rolling pin, roll each ball out thinly to a 14cm circle.

Divide the beef filling between the rounds of dough, spooning about 3 tbsp filling into the centre of each round. Brush the edges lightly with melted butter and fold over to make semi-circles, as if you're making pasties. Carefully press the edges together, then crimp with a fork to seal.

Lay the runzas on 2 baking trays lined with baking parchment. Brush them with the remaining melted butter and leave to prove for a final 20 minutes. Meanwhile, preheat the oven to 210°C/Fan 190°C/Gas 7.

Bake the runzas for 15–20 minutes until they are golden brown and crisp. Serve immediately.

BLUE CHEESE TART

This lovely tart makes a great lunch with a crisp green salad. I love using some ground toasted hazelnuts in the pastry, as the flavour goes beautifully with the blue cheese and gives an extra dimension to the finished dish. To make the cheese easier to grate, try putting it in the freezer for 15 minutes first. SERVES 6–8

For the pastry
30g shelled hazelnuts
170g plain flour, plus extra
 for dusting
1 tsp salt
120g butter, chilled and diced
1 egg yolk
3–4 tbsp iced water

For the filling
300ml double cream
6 egg yolks
2 tbsp thyme leaves
300g blue cheese (use your
 favourite), grated
Salt and freshly ground
 black pepper

Preheat the oven to 180°C/Fan 160°C/Gas 4. Scatter the nuts on a baking sheet and toast in the oven for 10–12 minutes, until the skins are blistered. Wrap in a clean tea towel and let steam for a few minutes, then rub in the cloth to remove the skins (as much as you can). Cool and grind with a pestle and mortar or pulse to a powder in a food processor; don't over-process.

To make the pastry, put the flour, ground nuts and salt into a food processor. Add the butter and pulse briefly until the mixture resembles coarse breadcrumbs. Add the egg yolk and blend briefly, adding the cold water a little at a time and mixing only until you achieve a soft, smooth dough. Wrap in cling film and rest in the fridge for at least 1 hour.

Heat the oven to 170°C/Fan 150°C/Gas 3½. Roll out the pastry on a lightly floured surface to the thickness of a £1 coin and large enough to line a 20cm loose-bottomed tart tin. Line the tin with the pastry, gently pressing it against the edge of the tin and letting any excess fall over the sides. Line the pastry case with baking parchment and fill with dried or ceramic baking beans. Stand on a baking sheet. Bake for 15–20 minutes.

Take out the paper and beans and bake for a further 10–15 minutes, until the pastry case is golden brown, cooked through and crisp. Let cool on the baking sheet, then carefully trim away any excess pastry from the edges, using a small serrated knife. Reduce the oven temperature to 160°C/Fan 140°C/Gas 3.

For the filling, in a large bowl, whisk together the cream, egg yolks, thyme and some salt and pepper. Stir in the blue cheese. Pour the mixture into the tart case, still on the baking sheet. Bake for 35–40 minutes, until the filling is light golden and set. Remove from the oven and let cool in the tin for 20 minutes.

Carefully remove the tart from the tin and cut into wedges.

CORN DOGS

This recipe takes hot dogs to another level! I love these guys dipped in barbecue sauce or smothered in sweet mustard. You can also remove the skewers and stick the hot dogs in a bun with some homemade tomato ketchup (page 176). Best snack ever. You'll need 8-10 wooden skewers, pre-soaked in cold water for 30 minutes and dried.
SERVES 8–10

For the batter
130g plain flour
90g fine cornmeal
1 tbsp caster sugar
2 tsp baking powder
1 tsp cayenne pepper
1 tsp salt
30g lard, chilled and finely
    diced
175ml whole milk
1 egg

For the dogs
Vegetable oil, for deep-frying
8–10 frankfurters (the best
    quality you can find)
Flour, for dusting
Flaky sea salt, to finish

To make the batter, mix together the flour, cornmeal, sugar, baking powder, cayenne pepper, salt and lard in a large bowl until combined. In a separate bowl, beat the milk and egg together and gradually whisk this mixture into the dry ingredients until you have a smooth, loose batter.

Heat about a 15cm depth of oil in a deep-fat fryer to 180°C. Or use a large, deep pan, making sure it is no more than a third full, as the oil will bubble up ferociously when you add the corn dogs. Use a frying thermometer to check the temperature, if you have one; otherwise drop a cube of dry white bread into the hot oil to test it – if the bread turns golden brown in just under a minute, the oil is up to temperature. Keep a close eye on it and never leave the pan unattended, even for a minute.

While the oil is heating up, drain the frankfurters and pat dry with kitchen paper. Thread a wooden skewer lengthways into (but not right through) each one, then dust with flour, shaking off any excess.

You will need to fry the corn dogs in batches. Don't overcrowd the pan, and let the oil come back up to temperature between batches. Dip the dogs into the batter, turning to coat evenly, and use tongs to gently lower them into the hot oil. Deep-fry for 3-4 minutes until golden brown, turning them throughout cooking, to ensure they colour evenly and the batter gets crisp.

Carefully remove the corn dogs from the oil using tongs or a slotted spoon and drain on a tray lined with kitchen paper. Keep hot while frying the remaining dogs.

Scatter the corn dogs with a sprinkling of sea salt and serve them immediately.

BUFFALO CHICKEN WINGS

Hot or cold, these are such a great snack, and they work brilliantly as a starter or as part of a big barbecue platter too. Don't be put off by the long list of ingredients. If you are missing a couple of the herbs or spices, just leave them out. I like to brine my chicken wings, to achieve a deeper flavour, but you can skip that process if you wish – they'll still be delicious. SERVES 4–6

1.5kg chicken wings
Vegetable oil, for oiling
    the tray(s)

For the brine
1 litre water
200g flaky sea salt
190g demerara sugar
1 tbsp black peppercorns
2 cloves
1 bay leaf
1 thyme sprig

For the rub
2½ tsp smoked paprika
2 tsp salt
1 tsp soft dark brown sugar
½ tsp ground cumin
½ tsp freshly ground black
    pepper
½ tsp ground coriander
½ tsp garlic powder
½ tsp cayenne pepper
½ tsp dried oregano
½ tsp dried thyme

For the glaze
75g butter
75g cider vinegar
75ml Tabasco sauce

To make the brine, put all of the ingredients into a large saucepan and bring to the boil, stirring to make sure the sugar and salt dissolve completely. Leave the brine to cool to room temperature and then chill in the fridge.

Once the brine is chilled, add the chicken wings. Cover and leave in the fridge for at least 2 hours, preferably longer. If you have time, brine them for 6–8 hours so they take on a stronger, more intense flavour.

Remove the chicken wings from the brine, drain and pat dry using kitchen paper.

Preheat the oven to 160°C/Fan 140°C/Gas 3.

Lightly oil 2 medium or 1 large non-stick baking tray(s).

To make the rub, mix together all the ingredients in a large bowl. Add the chicken wings and toss each one thoroughly in the spices, making sure they are all evenly coated.

Transfer the chicken wings to the baking tray(s), arranging them in a single layer. Bake in the oven for 40–45 minutes, until they're cooked through.

Turn the oven up to 200°C/Fan 180°C/Gas 6 and bake the chicken wings for a further 10 minutes until they're golden brown and crisp.

When you turn the oven up, make the glaze. Combine the butter, cider vinegar and Tabasco in a small saucepan. Bring to the boil over a high heat, then lower the heat and cook for 5–10 minutes or until it has thickened into a glossy glaze.

For the blue cheese dressing
250g strong blue cheese
200ml soured cream
100g mayonnaise
A splash of milk
A pinch of cayenne pepper
Salt and freshly ground
    black pepper

To serve
1 green chilli, sliced
6–8 celery sticks (strings
    removed with a vegetable
    peeler), cut into batons
A selection of pickles, ideally
    including pickled green
    chillies and pickled
    carrots (page 149)

Meanwhile, for the blue cheese dressing, crumble the cheese into a bowl, add the soured cream and mayonnaise and mix together. Loosen with a splash of milk until you reach the desired consistency, then stir in the cayenne pepper. Taste and season with salt and pepper if required.

Remove the chicken wings from the oven and, while they're still warm, pour over the spicy glaze. Use a spoon to coat and roll them in the glaze evenly. They should be nice and glossy.

Transfer the glazed wings to a serving board or platter and scatter with the sliced green chilli. Serve hot or cold with some crisp celery and pickles alongside.

WALDORF SALAD

This is such a top – yet simple – salad. I love the clean, crisp flavours that kick on through it, from the mild bitterness of the frisée and the peppery watercress, through the sweet apples and grapes, to the salty cheese. Its distinct flavours work very well in hot weather at barbecues, but because they're quite powerful and nutty, it works equally as well as an autumn or winter salad. SERVES 4–6

150g shelled walnuts

4 celery sticks

1 Romaine lettuce, thickly sliced

A bunch of watercress, thicker stems removed

A couple of handfuls of frisée (the tender pale leaves from the centre)

100g seedless white grapes, halved

About 2 tbsp flat-leaf parsley leaves

2 tbsp raisins

200g strong, salty blue cheese such as Roquefort, crumbled

2 sweet, crisp red apples

For the dressing

2 tbsp Dijon mustard

2 tbsp white wine vinegar

2 tbsp plain yoghurt

100ml olive oil

Salt and freshly ground black pepper

Preheat the oven to 180°C/Fan 160°C/Gas 4. Scatter the walnuts on a baking sheet and toast in the oven for 6–9 minutes until fragrant; be careful not to let them burn. Transfer to a plate and let cool slightly, then crumble roughly.

Using a vegetable peeler, peel away the strings from the celery, then slice the stalks thinly.

For the dressing, in a bowl, whisk the mustard, wine vinegar and yoghurt together, then gradually whisk in the olive oil until everything is well combined. Season with salt and pepper to taste.

Place the salad leaves in a large mixing bowl. Add the celery, toasted walnuts, grapes, parsley and raisins and toss together. Add the crumbled blue cheese to the bowl.

At the last minute (so they don't discolour), cut the apples into thin batons and add to the salad. Pour on the dressing and toss until evenly coated. Serve immediately.

CHEDDAR & ALE SOUP

This is a super soup – ideal on its own with some bread for lunch, or as part of a bigger meal. I really like the combination of the rich, hoppy ale and the gentle acidity from the dairy. The chopped apple and malty dressing I use to garnish the soup cuts through the rich flavours and really makes them shine. SERVES 4

75g butter
1 large onion (about 175g), diced
1 large potato (about 175g), peeled and diced
70g plain flour
500ml chicken stock
500ml brown ale (your choice, but the stronger the better)
100ml double cream
350g strong Cheddar cheese, grated
Salt and freshly ground black pepper

For the dressing
4 tbsp olive oil
1 tbsp malt extract
1 tbsp cider vinegar

To garnish
1 large Bramley apple, peeled, cored and finely diced
2 tbsp chopped chives

Melt the butter in a large, heavy-based saucepan over a medium heat. Add the onion and potato and cook gently, stirring from time to time, until softened (but don't let them take on any colour), around 10–15 minutes.

Sprinkle the flour evenly over the vegetables in the pan and cook, stirring, for 1–2 minutes, then stir in the chicken stock. Whack up the heat and bring to the boil, then reduce to a simmer and cook gently for about 10 minutes until the soup has thickened. Pour in the ale and heat gently for a further few minutes.

Remove from the heat, let cool slightly and then transfer the mixture to a blender or food processor. Add the cream and whiz until nice and smooth.

Pass the soup through a fine sieve into a clean saucepan and season with pepper and a little salt – do not add too much at this stage as the cheese will introduce extra saltiness later.

To make the dressing, whisk together the olive oil, malt extract and cider vinegar in a small bowl until emulsified.

Warm the soup gently over a low heat and stir in the grated Cheddar, allowing it to melt. Taste and adjust the seasoning if necessary.

Ladle the soup into warmed bowls and trickle a little dressing on top of each one. Sprinkle on the diced apple and chives and serve immediately.

CHICKEN & MATZO BALL SOUP

This cosy chicken soup with dumplings and noodles bobbing in it is so comforting. I make the dumplings from blitzed-up matzo crackers, which you can buy in lots of supermarkets and delis now. Like breadcrumbs, they make wonderful dumplings which absorb loads of flavour from the broth. In this recipe, I use a cooked chicken, but you could easily poach skinned raw pieces of chicken in the broth instead – just add them earlier in the cooking process and make sure they are cooked through before serving. SERVES 4–6

For the matzo balls

150g matzo crackers
1 tsp bicarbonate of soda
1 tsp ground cinnamon
½ tsp salt
1 tbsp finely chopped thyme
    leaves
4 eggs, separated
80ml olive oil, plus a little
    extra for oiling
40ml water

For the soup

2 tbsp vegetable oil
1 large onion, diced
1 large carrot, diced
1 large parsnip, diced
3 celery sticks (tough strings
    removed with a vegetable
    peeler), diced
6 garlic cloves, finely grated
1 chicken (about 1.4kg),
    roasted and chilled
1.2 litres chicken stock
1 tsp dried thyme
1 tsp dried sage
100g dried egg noodles
Salt and freshly ground
    black pepper

For the matzo balls, grind the crackers to a fine crumb using a food processor, or put them into a plastic bag and bash them with a rolling pin until they are finely crushed.

In a large bowl, stir together the matzo crumbs, bicarbonate of soda, cinnamon, salt and thyme. In a jug, whisk the egg yolks, olive oil and water together, then stir into the dry ingredients.

In a separate, large bowl, whisk the egg whites until they form soft peaks. Gently fold into the matzo mixture, using a spatula, until evenly combined and you have a thick batter. Cover with cling film and leave to rest in the fridge for a couple of hours.

Once chilled, get ready to roll the mixture into balls. Lightly oil your hands with a splash of oil - this will prevent the mixture from sticking and make it easier to shape. Roll the dough into 12 balls, roughly the size of golf balls. Arrange them on a tray or large plate and cover with cling film. Chill in the fridge for at least 30 minutes while you prepare the soup.

To make the chicken soup, heat the oil in a large saucepan over a medium-low heat. Add the onion and cook gently for 4–5 minutes, to soften. Add the carrot, parsnip, celery and garlic and continue to cook over a gentle heat for 10–15 minutes, until softened, stirring from time to time.

Meanwhile, tear the roasted chicken into large chunks and discard the skin.

Pour the chicken stock into the pan, bring to the boil and then lower the heat to a gentle simmer. Throw in the dried thyme and sage and season well with salt and pepper. Cook gently for around 10-15 minutes.

Remove the matzo balls from the fridge and add to the soup. Allow to poach very gently in the broth for 15-20 minutes. Add the noodles and cook for a further 10 minutes.

Finally, add the shredded chicken to the pan. If you'd prefer the soup to be less thick, add a little more chicken stock at this stage too. Carefully stir through the soup and cook gently for a few minutes until the chicken is nicely warmed through.

Ladle the soup into warmed bowls and serve immediately.

BORSCHT

Stunning, with deep, earthy flavours, this soup is quick and easy to make. Its history is rich and complex, with different versions originating from Russia and all over Eastern Europe. I'm giving you my proper dressed up version here, luxuriously garnished with caviar and duck – I confess it's the cheaper avruga caviar, made from herring roe, but it's a nice touch. If you want to pare it down a bit, garnish simply with soured cream. I love the soup's vibrant colour – I just try to remember not to wear white when eating it... SERVES 6–8

1 white cabbage, cored and
    finely shredded
500g peeled raw beetroot
    (prepared weight), grated
50g butter
1 large white onion, halved
    and thinly sliced
2 tbsp caraway seeds
200ml white wine
1 litre chicken stock
Juice of 1 lemon
2 tbsp red wine vinegar
1 tbsp thyme leaves
Salt and freshly ground
    black pepper

To garnish
Soured cream
Avruga caviar (optional)
Some leftover meat from
    slow-cooked duck legs
    (if you have it)
Soft thyme leaves

Bring a large saucepan of salted water to the boil. Add the cabbage and beetroot and blanch for 5 minutes. Using a slotted spoon, remove the vegetables from the pan and place on a tray or baking sheet lined with kitchen paper or a clean tea towel to drain; reserve the cooking water.

In a separate, large, heavy-based saucepan, melt the butter over a medium-low heat. Once it's foaming, add the onion and cook gently, stirring from time to time, for about 10 minutes until softened, but without letting it take on any colour. Stir in the caraway seeds and sweat for a further 1–2 minutes.

Pour in the wine and allow it to bubble away and reduce by half, then add the cabbage and beetroot. Pour in the chicken stock and top up with some of the reserved cooking liquid if necessary to cover the vegetables. Bring to the boil over a high heat, then lower the heat and simmer for 5 minutes.

Stir in the lemon juice, wine vinegar and thyme leaves. Season to taste with salt and pepper and adjust the consistency with more of the reserved cooking liquid if necessary.

Ladle the soup into warmed bowls and top with spoonfuls of soured cream. Spoon on some caviar and shredded, cooked duck if you're feeling extra indulgent, and scatter over some thyme leaves.

FISH & SHELLFISH

When it comes to everyday cooking, fish is your friend. In a few minutes, you can create something really fantastic, which looks and tastes far more impressive than the amount of effort you need to put in.

It's all about learning to understand your key ingredients and bringing out their special qualities. Meaty king prawns, with their robust texture and slightly sweet flesh, can take strong flavours. Try the spicy king prawns with guacamole and salsa and you'll see what I mean – the prawns are brilliant with the zesty salsa, crunchy iceberg and creamy avocado. It's all about creating great contrasts.

With more subtle-tasting and delicately textured fish, you need a lighter touch – look to introduce harmonious flavourings that make the dish shine. This is where you can go to town with citrus, some of the softer herbs and lovely veg like fennel. Try rainbow trout with pine nut dressing or pollack with orange and dill; both of these show how to achieve a great balance of flavours.

If it's a speedy dish you're after, you can't do better than spaghetti with clam sauce or Portuguese mussel stew. I guarantee you'll have a brilliant meal on the table faster than you could get a takeaway. Both dishes are easy enough for a weeknight supper, but good enough to dish up for a special weekend dinner too.

Then, just for fun, I've included crayfish 'popcorn'. Crispy, crunchy and moreish, you can serve these as a starter, snack or meal on their own with some salad and a nice bowl of mayonnaise or Marie Rose sauce – a guaranteed crowd pleaser, that one.

I know some people fret about cooking fish and shellfish, but I do hope you'll have a go at these recipes. The secret is not to worry too much – just relax and enjoy yourself. The most important thing is to keep a close eye on it during cooking, to avoid overdoing it. All fish and seafood keep cooking and firming up a bit after you've plated them so you need to allow for this. Once you've cracked that, there's nothing holding you back.

SPICY KING PRAWNS WITH GUACAMOLE & SALSA

I love this combination of zesty, spicy salsa and big, meaty king prawns. The avocado offers a soft and creamy respite from the heat of the chilli, and crisp, cool iceberg lettuce adds texture. Fold it all up in a flour tortilla or wrap and get stuck in. SERVES 4

600g peeled raw king
    prawns, deveined
Vegetable oil, for frying

For the salsa
150ml red wine vinegar
50g caster sugar
300ml passata
1 red onion, halved
4-5 spring onions, trimmed
½ cucumber
Finely grated zest and juice
    of 3 unwaxed limes
½ bunch each of coriander
    and mint, chopped
3 garlic cloves, finely grated
2 red chillies, finely diced
2 tbsp chopped salted
    anchovies

For the guacamole
2 ripe avocados
2 plum tomatoes
3 tbsp lemon juice
2 tbsp chopped coriander
2 tbsp Worcestershire sauce
1 tbsp soured cream

To serve
8 flour tortillas
A handful of shredded
    iceberg lettuce
1 red chilli, sliced into rings

First cook the prawns. Warm a deep sauté pan over a high heat and add a glug of oil. Drop the prawns into the pan and sauté quickly for 1–2 minutes on each side, ensuring they are seared all over, bright pink and cooked through. With a slotted spoon, remove to a plate. Put to one side.

Return the pan to the heat, add the wine vinegar and sugar, and stir to dissolve the sugar. Let bubble for a few minutes until reduced to a glaze. Pour in the passata, bring to the boil, then reduce the heat and simmer gently for about 10 minutes until reduced by a third. Remove from the heat and let cool.

Finely slice the red and spring onions and place in a large bowl. Halve the cucumber lengthways, deseed and dice, then add to the bowl with the lime zest and juice, coriander, mint, garlic, chillies (including the seeds if you like the heat) and anchovies. Stir in the passata mix, check the seasoning and add some salt and pepper if necessary. Set the salsa aside.

To make the guacamole, halve and stone the avocados and scoop the flesh from the skins into a large bowl. Skin, deseed and dice the tomatoes (see page 14) and add to the bowl. Add the lemon juice, coriander, Worcestershire sauce and soured cream. Mash together with a fork until fairly smooth and creamy, but still retaining some texture. Season to taste with salt and pepper.

Arrange the tortillas on a flat surface and spread evenly with the guacamole. Spoon on the salsa and cover with the shredded lettuce. Scatter over the sliced chilli, arrange the prawns on top and fold up tightly to create delicious wraps. Enjoy immediately!

CRAYFISH 'POPCORN'

American signal crayfish are now the most common crayfish in British waters. They're easy to get hold of fresh, or you can buy the prepared tail meat from your fishmonger or supermarket. The cornmeal coating batter I've used here gives them great crunch. These crayfish 'popcorn' are ideal party food with some mayonnaise to dip them into, or you can serve them as a seafood cocktail starter dressed in Marie Rose sauce. SERVES 8

500g crayfish tail meat, cleaned
Vegetable oil, for deep-frying
Plain flour, for dusting

For the batter
200g fine cornmeal
100g tapioca flour
1 tsp garlic powder
1 tsp freshly ground black pepper
1 tsp cayenne pepper
½ tsp bicarbonate of soda
330ml sparkling water, ice cold

To serve
A pinch of smoked paprika
A pinch of sea salt
1 unwaxed pink grapefruit, for zesting
Some good mayonnaise or lime and paprika mayo (page 47), for dipping

Pat the crayfish tails dry with kitchen paper and set aside.

Heat about a 12cm depth of oil in a deep-fat fryer to 180°C. Or use a large, deep pan, making sure it is no more than a third full as the oil will bubble up ferociously when you add the crayfish. Use a frying thermometer to check the temperature, if you have one; otherwise drop a cube of dry white bread into the hot oil to test it – if the bread turns golden brown in just under a minute, the oil is up to temperature. Keep a close eye on it and never leave the pan unattended, even for a minute.

While the oil is heating, make the batter. In a large bowl, mix together the cornmeal, tapioca flour, garlic power, black pepper, cayenne pepper and bicarbonate of soda. Whisk in the sparkling water to form a smooth, loose batter.

Dust the crayfish in flour to coat evenly, but shake off any excess. You will need to fry them in batches. Don't overcrowd the pan, and allow the oil to come back up to temperature between batches. Dip the crayfish into the batter to coat, then lower them into the hot oil and deep-fry for 2–3 minutes until golden brown and crisp.

Carefully remove the crayfish 'popcorn' from the oil using a slotted spoon and drain on a tray lined with kitchen paper. Repeat with the remaining crayfish.

Pile the crayfish 'popcorn' up high in a bowl and season with a pinch of smoked paprika and a little salt to taste. Finely grate some of the grapefruit zest on top of the popcorn, being careful to avoid adding any of the white pith. Serve immediately, with some mayonnaise to dip them into.

QUEEN SCALLOPS WITH LIME & PAPRIKA MAYO

These beautiful little scallops are a smaller species than the king scallops you would typically be served in a restaurant, and they have a sweeter flavour. If you have trouble finding them, this recipe works with regular scallops too – in this case, allow 3–5 per person. Always buy fresh scallops in the shell, not frozen ones, and ask the fishmonger to clean them for you, keeping the coral on. SERVES 4

30–40 queen scallops,
    cleaned and trimmed but
    with the coral still on
150g plain flour
50g tapioca flour
1 tbsp smoked paprika
A pinch of salt
Vegetable oil, for frying
100g butter, diced
Juice of 1–2 lemons

For the lime & paprika mayo
3 egg yolks
1 tbsp Dijon mustard
1 tbsp white wine vinegar
Finely grated zest and juice
    of 2 unwaxed limes
2 tsp smoked paprika
1 tsp salt
500ml vegetable oil
Freshly ground black or
    white pepper (optional)

To serve
1 unwaxed lime, for zesting
Lime wedges

First prepare the mayo. Put the egg yolks, mustard, wine vinegar, lime zest and juice, smoked paprika and salt into a small food processor and pulse to blend. With the motor still running, add the oil, a drip at a time at first and then more quickly once you've added about half the oil. It will emulsify and thicken. Taste and adjust the seasoning, then pass through a sieve into a bowl. Cover and refrigerate until needed.

To prepare the scallops, mix together the flours, smoked paprika and salt in a bowl. Pat the scallops dry with kitchen paper and drop them into the flour mixture. Toss to coat evenly, shaking off any excess.

Warm a glug of oil in a medium-large, non-stick frying pan over a high heat. You may need to fry the scallops in batches, to avoid overcrowding the pan. Cook for just 30–60 seconds on each side before flipping them over. (If using king scallops, fry for 1–2 minutes per side.)

Towards the end of cooking, add the butter to the pan, allow to foam and turn nutty brown and use to baste the scallops as they finish cooking. Squeeze a little lemon juice over the scallops and remove them from the pan.

Serve the scallops immediately, with a sprinkling of lime zest, the lime and paprika mayo and lime wedges.

You'll have more mayonnaise than you need. Keep the rest in a sealed jar in the fridge for up to 5 days, to eat with prawns, crayfish 'popcorn' (page 44) or crab cakes (page 48).

CRAB CAKES

Crab cakes are the ultimate fish cake. It's important to use the finest fresh crab you can find – the fresher the meat, the sweeter it will taste. If you have time, cook your own crab and pick the meat yourself as this is the best way to ensure the biggest flakes possible. MAKES 8

1 red pepper, cored, deseeded
   and finely diced
1 small onion, finely chopped
4 spring onions, finely sliced
2 garlic cloves, finely grated
½ bunch of parsley, tough
   stems removed, leaves
   chopped
Finely grated zest of
   1 unwaxed lemon
2 tbsp Dijon mustard
2 tsp Worcestershire sauce
½ tsp Tabasco sauce
1–2 tsp salt
1 tsp cayenne pepper
1 egg, plus 1 extra egg white,
   lightly beaten together
500g white crabmeat,
   freshly picked over
200g fresh breadcrumbs
Plain flour, for dusting
Vegetable oil and butter,
   for cooking
Juice of ½ lemon

To serve
Mayonnaise, or lime and
   paprika mayo (page 47)

To make the crab cakes, put the red pepper, onion, spring onions, garlic, parsley, lemon zest, all of the seasonings and the beaten egg into a large bowl. Mix together with your hands to ensure all the ingredients are evenly combined.

Gently fold in the crabmeat and 75g of the breadcrumbs. Stir through carefully, just to combine. You don't want to mash the delicate crab flesh. Cover and chill in the fridge for 30 minutes to firm up – this will make it easier to form the mixture into crab cakes later.

Divide the crab mixture into 8 equal portions then, using lightly floured hands, shape and mould into patties. Transfer the crab cakes to a tray, cover with cling film and chill in the fridge for at least an hour.

When you're ready to cook the crab cakes, sprinkle the remaining breadcrumbs onto a flat tray or plate. Carefully roll each crab cake in the crumbs on both sides to coat evenly. Gently shake off any excess breadcrumbs.

Heat a generous glug of oil in a large, non-stick frying pan over a medium-high heat. You may need to fry the crab cakes in a couple of batches, to avoid overcrowding the pan. Cook the cakes in the pan for 3–4 minutes on each side until they are golden brown, cooked through and deliciously crisp.

Towards the end of cooking, add a generous knob of butter to the pan and melt until foaming and a rich golden brown. Squeeze in the lemon juice and baste the crab cakes by spooning over the nutty butter and juices.

Transfer to a warmed plate and serve with plenty of mayonnaise and a crisp green salad.

PORTUGUESE MUSSEL STEW

This is a lovely, vibrant and colourful dish, with great texture and flavour. The bigger mussels you can find the better! They're so quick and easy to prepare and are great for soaking up the flavours of everything else they're cooked with. Here, the chorizo's fat and spices are a great seasoning for the sweet and milky mussel meat. SERVES 4

2kg fresh mussels in their shells
8 tomatoes
4 tbsp olive oil
300g cooking chorizo, thickly sliced
1 onion, diced
4 garlic cloves, finely grated
1 green pepper, cored, deseeded and diced
2 green chillies, chopped (seeds and all)
3 tbsp plain flour
450ml white wine
A bunch of flat-leaf parsley, tough stems removed, leaves finely chopped
Salt and freshly ground black pepper

First clean the mussels. Discard any with broken shells or any that don't snap shut when you tap them firmly. Pull off the beards and scrape off any large barnacles on the shells, using the back of a knife. Rinse the mussels under cold running water to remove any dirt or grit. Refrigerate until ready to cook.

Skin, deseed and dice the tomatoes (see page 14); set aside until needed.

Heat the olive oil in a large saucepan over a medium-low heat. Add the chorizo and sweat gently for a few minutes, stirring frequently, until the chorizo has released some of its tasty red oil. Add the onion and garlic and continue to cook gently for a further 4–5 minutes to soften. Throw in the diced pepper and chillies and sauté for a few more minutes.

Sprinkle the flour into the pan and cook gently for a couple of minutes, stirring all the time, to cook out the flour.

Pour in the white wine and cook for a few minutes longer, stirring from time to time, until the mixture has thickened. Throw the cleaned mussels into the pot, cover with a tight-fitting lid and allow the mussels to steam for 8–10 minutes over a medium heat until all of the shells have opened and they're cooked through. Discard any mussels that remain shut.

Stir in the diced tomatoes and chopped parsley. Check the seasoning and add some salt and pepper if necessary.

Ladle the mussel stew into warm serving bowls, making sure that everyone has an even helping of both mussels and chorizo. Serve with some lovely crusty bread to soak up all the delicious juices.

CLAM CHOWDER

This rich and soothing soup is usually associated with New England, but it sits very easily on these shores too. Simple to make and with layers of big flavour, this recipe gives you a lot back for the small amount of work you need to put in. Feel free to swap the clams for mussels if you prefer. I like to garnish the chowder with a handful of good pork scratchings, for a bit of added texture and taste. SERVES 4–6

2kg fresh clams in their
    shells
400ml water
250g lardons or diced bacon
1 large onion, diced
100g butter, chilled and diced
30g plain flour
750ml whole milk, warmed
    (but not boiling)
2 medium potatoes, peeled
    and diced (about 300g
    prepared weight)
6 tbsp chopped flat-leaf
    parsley leaves
Salt and freshly ground
    black pepper

To serve
100g pork scratchings,
    bashed up

First, clean the clams carefully. Discard any with broken shells, or any that are open and don't snap shut when you tap them. Wash the clams in a colander or bowl under cold running water to remove any dirt and grit. This may take a while – you need to run the water long enough to clean them properly.

Heat a large saucepan over a high heat. Add the clams, pour on the 400ml water and quickly cover with a tight-fitting lid. Cook for 5–8 minutes, until all of the clams have opened up. Meanwhile, line a large colander with a clean tea towel or a piece of muslin and set it over a large bowl or jug.

Once the clams have opened, remove the pan from the heat. Drain the clams in the muslin-lined colander and reserve the cooking liquor to use later.

Once cool enough to handle, pick the clams from the shells, discarding any that remain shut as they are unsafe to eat. Discard the empty clam shells too. Roughly chop the clam meat and set aside.

Warm a large saucepan over a low heat and add the lardons or bacon. Slowly render the fat and cook for about 10 minutes until the lardons crisp up and turn golden brown. Use a slotted spoon to remove them from the pan and set aside.

Add the onion to the rendered fat in the pan and cook gently, stirring from time to time, for about 10 minutes, until softened. Drop 30g of the butter into the pan and allow it to melt, then sprinkle on the flour. Stir over the heat for a couple of minutes to cook out the raw flour taste, then gradually stir in the reserved cooking liquid and warmed milk. Simmer for a few minutes until thickened slightly.

Add the diced potatoes to the pan and simmer gently for a further 10 minutes until they are almost tender. Stir in the lardons and chopped clams. Cook very gently over a low heat for 5 minutes, making sure you don't let it boil (or the milk will curdle the chowder).

Gradually stir in the remaining cubes of diced butter – this will thicken and enrich the chowder. Season with salt and pepper to taste and stir through most of the chopped parsley.

Ladle the chowder into warmed bowls and serve sprinkled with the crushed pork scratchings and remaining parsley.

SPAGHETTI WITH CLAM SAUCE

This is my version of that Italian classic, spaghetti vongole. Originally a Venetian peasant dish, it's now almost as famous as spaghetti bolognaise. I shell the clams to make more of a sauce rather than tossing them through the pasta – it's a bit more work to prepare, but it's way easier to eat! SERVES 6

2kg fresh clams in their shells

350ml white wine

1 dried chilli

100ml olive oil

75g butter

4 banana shallots, finely diced

6 garlic cloves, thinly sliced

2 tsp dried chilli flakes (or more if you fancy)

600g dried spaghetti

3–4 tbsp chopped flat-leaf parsley leaves

Salt and freshly ground black pepper

First, clean the clams (see page 52). Warm a deep saucepan over a high heat. Add the clams along with the wine and whole dried chilli and immediately cover with a tight-fitting lid. Steam for 5–8 minutes, until the clams have all opened up. Drain the clams in a muslin-lined colander over a bowl or jug (see page 52) and reserve the cooking liquor to use later.

Once the clams are cool enough to handle, pick the meat from the shells and place in a bowl. Discard any clams that remain shut as these are not safe to eat. Discard the empty shells.

Heat the olive oil and butter in a deep sauté pan or saucepan over a low heat until the butter has melted. Add the shallots and garlic and cook gently for 8–10 minutes, stirring from time to time, until softened.

Whack up the heat and pour in the reserved clam liquor. Bring to the boil then lower the heat and let the liquid emulsify with the butter. It should be lovely and glossy and have thickened slightly. Add the prepared clams to the pot, followed by the chilli flakes. Stir to combine.

Meanwhile, bring a large saucepan of salted water to the boil. Cook the spaghetti for 10–12 minutes until *al dente* (cooked but still with a bite).

Drain the pasta in a colander, reserving a cupful of the cooking water. Tip the pasta into the pot of clams and toss to combine, loosening with a splash of the pasta water if necessary.

Season to taste with salt and pepper and stir in the chopped parsley. Serve at once, in warmed bowls.

PRAWN & CHICKEN GUMBO

Gumbo is a similar style of one-pot wonder to a good bouillabaisse. Created by the Creoles in South Louisiana at the turn of the nineteenth century, it remains just as popular today as it was then. Of course, there are many variations. Don't be put off by the lengthy list of ingredients – once they're in the pan, it's not a complicated recipe. It's just full of flavour, so give it a go. SERVES 8

2 large boneless chicken breasts, skinned
100ml vegetable oil
8 chicken thighs, bone in and skin on
4 rashers of smoked streaky bacon, diced
500g smoked sausage or chorizo, cut into 1cm slices
100g plain flour
2 tsp cayenne pepper
2 tsp smoked paprika
1 large onion, diced
2 green peppers, cored, deseeded and diced
4 celery sticks (tough strings removed), diced
8 garlic cloves, finely grated
4 bay leaves
A small bunch of thyme, tied with kitchen string
1 litre chicken stock
500ml tomato juice
200g okra, sliced into rings
250g peeled raw tiger prawns
4 spring onions, trimmed and sliced
½ bunch of parsley, stalks removed, leaves chopped
Salt and freshly ground black pepper

Cut each chicken breast into 4 even-sized pieces.

Heat the oil in a large, heavy-based saucepan over a medium-high heat. When hot, add the chicken thighs and breast pieces and sear for a few minutes until nicely browned. You may need to do this in batches to avoid overcrowding the pan. Remove the chicken from the pan and set aside on a large plate.

Return the pan to a medium heat, add the bacon and cook for a few minutes, stirring frequently, until golden and crisp. Remove with a slotted spoon and set aside with the chicken.

Now add the sausage slices to the pan and allow them to colour and release their oil. Once browned, remove them from the pan with a slotted spoon and set aside, with the chicken and bacon.

Place the pan back over a low heat and add the flour – there may be quite a lot of fat in the pan at this stage, but don't worry. Cook, stirring constantly, for around 8–10 minutes to cook out the flour and make a thick, smooth paste. Once the paste takes on a dark golden brown colour, add the cayenne pepper and smoked paprika and cook for a further minute.

Add the onion, peppers, celery and garlic to the pan. Stir, increase the heat and cook for a few minutes to soften the vegetables. Throw in the bay leaves and thyme.

Return the chicken pieces, bacon and sausage to the pan, along with any juices that have accumulated on the plate.

Pour in the chicken stock and tomato juice and bring to the boil. Lower the heat and simmer gently for around 1 hour until thickened, stirring from time to time. Remove the thyme.

Stir in the okra and cook gently for 8–10 minutes. Now add the prawns and cook for 2–3 minutes until they turn bright pink and are cooked through. Stir in the sliced spring onions and chopped parsley, heat through for a minute then season well with salt and pepper.

Ladle the gumbo into warmed bowls and serve either just as it is or with some steamed rice.

SOUSED KING PRAWNS

Meaty prawns taste so good after a couple of days in this sousing liquor. You can either serve them with some rye crackers or toasted sourdough, or turn them into a salad. Simply toss some big cos lettuce leaves with spoonfuls of the prawns and use the sousing liquid as the acidic part of a vinaigrette, whisking in some more olive oil until you get the balance of flavour you like. SERVES 6–8, OR MORE AS A STARTER

1.5kg peeled raw king prawns (tail shell intact), deveined

For the cooking liquor
3 celery sticks, thinly sliced
1 unwaxed lemon, thinly sliced
2 tbsp salt
1 tbsp black peppercorns, tied in muslin with kitchen string
About 2 litres water

For the sousing liquor
1 small onion, thinly sliced into rings
3 celery sticks (tough strings removed with a vegetable peeler), thinly sliced
10 garlic cloves, sliced
6 tbsp capers
10 bay leaves
4 tsp fennel seeds
2 tsp celery salt
2 tsp crushed pink peppercorns
2 tsp cracked black pepper
10 dashes of Tabasco sauce
600ml white wine vinegar
1 tbsp salt
700ml olive oil

For the cooking liquor, put the celery, lemon slices, salt and bundle of peppercorns into a large saucepan and pour in the 2 litres cold water. Put the lid on the pan and bring to the boil over a medium-high heat. Turn down the heat so the water is simmering.

Immediately add the prawns, stirring, then take off the heat and cover with the lid. Leave the prawns to poach gently in the residual heat of the liquid for 8–10 minutes until they are bright pink and cooked through.

Remove the prawns with a slotted spoon; discard the cooking liquor and aromatics. Once the prawns have cooled, pat dry using kitchen paper and transfer to a large bowl.

For the sousing liquor, add the onion, celery, garlic, capers, bay leaves, fennel seeds, celery salt, pink and black pepper, and the Tabasco to the prawns. Toss well to distribute the flavourings evenly.

Put the wine vinegar and salt into a jug blender or food processor and whiz to dissolve the salt, then add the olive oil and whiz together again, until the mixture thickens and emulsifies. It should have a lovely glossy sheen to it and be nice and smooth. Pour over the prawns and flavourings in the bowl, stirring to coat them evenly.

Spoon the prawns into cold, sterilised jars or lidded plastic containers. Seal and leave to souse in the fridge for 48 hours. Discard the bay leaves before serving.

The sousing liquid will separate after a while. Simply give the jar or container a shake from time to time to re-emulsify. Eat the prawns within 3 days of sousing.

PICKLED FISH

Lightly pickled fish is delicious served with toasted brown bread and creamed horseradish, as a tasty starter or lunch. I use mackerel here, but any oily fish will work just as well – try it with sardines, herring or red mullet. You can get your fishmonger to fillet the fish for you. SERVES 5, OR 10 AS A STARTER

10 mackerel fillets, skin on
  and pin-boned

For the cure mix
1 tsp coriander seeds
1 tsp fennel seeds
1 tsp mustard seeds
1 tsp black peppercorns
1 clove
50g caster sugar
50g flaky sea salt

For the pickling liquor
200ml water
100ml white wine vinegar
80g caster sugar
Finely pared zest and juice
  of 2 unwaxed oranges
Finely pared zest and juice
  of 1 unwaxed lemon
Finely pared zest and juice
  of 2 unwaxed limes

For the vegetables
1 carrot
2 red onions
2 celery sticks (tough strings
  removed with a vegetable
  peeler)
2 small turnips
6 French breakfast radishes
1 unwaxed lime, thinly sliced

For the cure mix, grind together the coriander, fennel and mustard seeds, black peppercorns and clove, using an electric spice grinder or pestle and mortar, to as fine a powder as you can. Pass through a fine sieve into a bowl and stir in the sugar and salt.

Coat the mackerel fillets evenly in the cure mix, pressing it gently into the flesh. Lay the fillets on a large plate, cover with cling film and chill in the fridge for 3 hours.

Meanwhile, prepare the pickling liquor. Put the water, wine vinegar and sugar into a medium saucepan and heat, stirring to dissolve the sugar and salt. Bring to the boil, then add the citrus zests and juices. Continue to boil for a couple of minutes, then lower the heat and simmer, uncovered, for 5–10 minutes. Remove from the heat.

Thinly slice all of the vegetables and the lime and place in a large, sealable plastic or glass container, deep enough to hold the liquor and fish. Pour over the pickling liquor, stir to distribute the vegetables evenly and allow to cool.

Once the fish has cured for 3 hours, remove it from the fridge. Rinse it briefly under cold running water and pat dry with kitchen paper.

Add the fish to the container with the pickling liquor and vegetables, making sure it's all nicely submerged. Cover with a lid and refrigerate for 2 days before eating.

Eat within 2–3 days of pickling, with warm brown toast and creamed horseradish if you like.

SEARED SEA BASS WITH ROASTED PEPPER SALSA

Roasting the peppers gives this salsa an extra layer of flavour. Together with the lime and herb soured cream, it works very well with sea bass or any other meaty fish, such as grey mullet or even tuna or salmon. Get your fishmonger to prepare the fish for you. SERVES 4

4 sea bass fillets, about 200g
   each, skin on, scaled and
   pin-boned
Plain flour, for dusting
Vegetable oil, for frying
A generous knob of butter
A squeeze of lemon juice
Salt and freshly ground
   black pepper

For the roasted pepper salsa
2 green peppers
8–10 tomatoes
½ cucumber
Vegetable oil, for frying
1 onion, finely diced
3 green chillies, chopped
   (seeds and all)
4 garlic cloves, finely grated
Finely grated zest and juice
   of 2 unwaxed limes
3 tbsp chopped coriander
   leaves and stems
2–3 tbsp olive oil

For the soured cream
150g soured cream
Finely grated zest of
   1 unwaxed lime
2 tbsp chopped mint leaves
2 tbsp chopped coriander
   stalks

First prepare the roasted pepper salsa. Place the green peppers on a baking tray and use a cook's blowtorch to carefully scorch them all over until they're blackened. If you don't have a blowtorch, you can do this under a fiercely hot grill or turn them on a fork directly over a gas ring.

Wrap the charred peppers in cling film or put them in a plastic bag, seal and allow to steam for 5 minutes. Unwrap and peel off the charred skins. Halve the peppers, remove the core and seeds, then cut into small chunks and place in a large bowl.

Skin, deseed and dice the tomatoes (see page 14) and add to the bowl with the peppers.

Halve the cucumber lengthways, deseed and dice. Heat a splash of oil in a medium frying pan over a high heat then add the cucumber and sauté quickly for a couple of minutes, until lightly browned. Remove from the heat and add to the bowl.

Return the pan to the heat and add a splash more oil. Throw in the onion and sauté over a high heat for around 5 minutes until softened and browned. Add to the bowl.

Add the chopped chillies, garlic (I like to keep it raw to give the salsa a bit more punch), lime zest and juice, coriander and olive oil to the bowl. Mix together and season with salt and pepper to taste. Set aside until ready to serve.

For the soured cream garnish, put all the ingredients into a small bowl and stir together to combine. Season to taste with salt and pepper then set aside until ready to serve.

To prepare the sea bass, use a sharp knife to make shallow, parallel incisions in the skin (don't cut into the flesh), to prevent it from curling up during cooking. Dust the fillets with flour and shake off any excess. Season with a little salt.

Heat a large, non-stick frying pan over a medium heat and add a splash of oil. When it is hot, lay the fillets in the pan skin side down and hold them in place until they have relaxed and the skin no longer wants to curl up. Cook for around 3–4 minutes, until the skin is crispy and the fish is almost cooked through.

Flip the fillets over, cook for another 1–2 minutes, then add a knob of butter and a little squeeze of lemon juice. Baste the fish with the buttery juices and remove from the heat.

Serve the seared bass on warmed plates with the salsa and soured cream alongside. The extra salsa will keep in the fridge for 1–2 days – enjoy as a snack with pitta or tortilla chips.

SUNFLOWER SEED CRUSTED SEA TROUT

Trout has a wonderful rich and earthy flavour. Coating the fillets with sunflower seeds enhances their depth of flavour; it also gives a lovely textural crunch to contrast with the soft flesh of the fish. Brushing the fish with the sweetened vinegar syrup lifts the dish to a whole new level. SERVES 6

6 sea trout fillets, about
    200g each
Vegetable oil, for frying
75g butter
Juice of 1 lemon

For the vinegar syrup
100ml white wine vinegar
100g caster sugar

For the sunflower seed crust
50g sunflower seeds
50g plain flour
50g coarse cornmeal
1 tsp salt
1 tsp cayenne pepper

First make the vinegar syrup. Put the wine vinegar and sugar in a small saucepan and bring to a simmer, stirring to dissolve the sugar. Increase the heat to high and boil for a few minutes to reduce until thickened and syrupy. Set aside to cool.

For the crust, toast the sunflower seeds in a small, dry frying pan over a medium heat, shaking the pan, for 2–3 minutes until they start to colour; be careful not to burn them. Tip onto a plate and let cool, then using a pestle and mortar, bash the seeds roughly, leaving some whole for an interesting texture.

Tip the flour and cornmeal into a large bowl and mix in the crushed sunflower seeds, salt and cayenne pepper.

Brush the trout fillets on both sides with the cooled vinegar syrup, then dip into the sunflower seed mixture, pressing it in gently to encase and coat the fillets evenly. Pat off any excess.

You may need to cook the trout fillets in batches, to avoid overcrowding the pan. Heat a large, non-stick frying pan over a medium heat and add a splash of oil. Once the oil is hot, place the trout fillets in the pan and gently hold them in place until they feel relaxed. Cook until the crust is golden brown and crisp, around 2–3 minutes. Don't be tempted to flip them over too soon, or the coating might come away from the fillets.

Carefully turn the fillets over and cook the other side, until the crust is golden and the flesh is soft and succulent. Towards the end of cooking, add the butter to the pan with a squeeze of lemon juice. Baste the fillets with the buttery juices. Remove the fillets from the pan and serve immediately, with the juices spooned over and buttered peas on the side, if you like.

BLACKENED CAJUN REDFISH

This recipe makes a lot of smoke and choke! Stick the extractor fan on full, open all the windows or cook it outside! It's worth the effort though, as the flavour is fantastic – sweet and spicy, charred and moist, all at the same time. It's an iconic Cajun dish that's just my kind of food. Serve it with any of your favourite barbecue relishes and salads. SERVES 6

6 red snapper fillets or
    dorado fillets, about 250g
    each, skin on and
    pin-boned
100g butter, melted

For the Cajun rub
1 tbsp sweet paprika
1 tbsp salt
2 tsp onion powder
1½ tsp garlic powder
1 tsp cayenne pepper
1 tsp freshly ground white
    pepper
1 tsp freshly ground black
    pepper
1 tsp dried oregano
½ tsp dried thyme

Bring the fish to room temperature. Using a sharp knife, cut a few shallow incisions into the skin of each fillet to help prevent it curling up during cooking. Don't cut too deeply – you only want to cut into the skin, not the flesh.

To make the Cajun rub, mix all the ingredients together in a bowl until evenly combined.

Brush the fish fillets with the melted butter to coat them all over then lay on a baking tray. Sprinkle over about 3 tbsp of the Cajun rub, gently patting it onto the fillets and making sure they're evenly covered on both sides. Gently shake off any excess.

You will need to cook the fish fillets in batches, to avoid overcrowding the pan. Heat a large, cast-iron skillet or heavy-based frying pan over a high heat until it's smoking hot.

Place a couple of fillets skin side down in the pan. Carefully hold them down by pressing with a fish slice or spatula until they have relaxed and no longer want to curl up. Cook until the skin is very well browned – almost black but not burnt! Depending how hot your pan is, this should take 3–4 minutes. You want the fish to be 90 per cent cooked through.

Carefully flip the fillets over with a fish slice and cook the other side for about 2 minutes until crisp. Remove to a plate and keep warm while you cook the rest of the fillets. Serve the fillets as soon as they are all cooked, on warmed plates.

POLLACK WITH ORANGE & DILL

The lovely, white flesh of pollack goes really well with a citrus dressing and the earthiness of the dill. I use a bit of Douglas fir in this dish, which might seem a bit 'cheffy' for everyday, but if you can get your hands on some, it's a fantastic addition and goes brilliantly with the other ingredients. If you can't, no worries. Just leave it out. I like to serve this with a simple potato salad. SERVES 4

4 pollack fillets, about 250g each
Vegetable oil, for frying
Flaky sea salt

For the dressing
3 unwaxed oranges
100ml olive oil
150ml cider vinegar
75g caster sugar
A small bunch of dill, chopped, a few sprigs saved for the garnish
2 tbsp Douglas fir pine needles, chopped (optional)

For the coating
175g coarse yellow cornmeal
40g plain flour
1 tsp salt
1 tsp cayenne pepper
1 tsp garlic powder

For the garnish
1 orange, peeled, all pith removed and cut into segments

First make the dressing. Pare the zest from 2 oranges with a vegetable peeler, keeping a little of the pith on, and cut into small dice. Place in a small saucepan, cover with the olive oil and heat very gently over a low heat, for 20 minutes or until the skin is just soft. Take off the heat and leave to cool.

Squeeze the juice from all the oranges and put into a small pan with the cider vinegar and sugar. Bring to the boil, stirring to dissolve the sugar. Let it bubble to reduce by two-thirds until thickened and syrupy. Pour into a bowl and allow to cool.

Add the orange zest and olive oil mix to the orange juice reduction and whisk to combine. Stir in the chopped dill and pine needles if using, and set aside until ready to serve.

For the fish coating, mix all the ingredients together in a large bowl. Heat about a 2cm depth of oil in a deep-sided frying pan or sauté pan until it reaches 180°C. Use a frying thermometer to check the temperature, if you have one; otherwise drop a cube of dry white bread into the hot oil to test it – if the bread turns golden brown in just under a minute, the oil is ready.

Dust the fish fillets on both sides with the cornmeal coating, shaking off any excess. You may need to fry them in batches, depending on the size of your pan. Lay the fish in the pan and fry for 2–3 minutes on each side until the crust is crisp and golden brown. Using a fish slice, carefully transfer to a tray lined with kitchen paper to drain. Season lightly with salt.

Serve the pollack fillets on warmed plates, garnished with the orange segments and dill, with the dressing spooned over.

RAINBOW TROUT WITH PINE NUT DRESSING

A fly-fished rainbow trout is a fantastic catch. It has a clean, mild flavour – not in any way 'dirty' or 'muddy' – which I really like. You could almost cook the fish on a riverbank, having just caught it... just bring a small camping stove and a few choice ingredients. SERVES 2

100g butter

75g pine nuts

Plain flour, for dusting

2 rainbow trout, filleted and butterflied (you can get your fishmonger to do this for you)

1 tbsp vegetable oil

2 hard-boiled eggs

75ml dry vermouth, such as Noilly Prat

Finely grated zest and juice of 1 unwaxed lemon

Pinch of freshly ground white pepper

2 tbsp chopped marjoram leaves

2 tbsp chopped parsley leaves

Salt and freshly ground black pepper

Melt a knob of the butter in a large, non-stick frying pan over a medium heat and add the pine nuts. Toast in the pan, shaking frequently, until they are evenly golden brown. Remove from the pan with a slotted spoon and set aside on a plate.

Season the flour with salt and pepper and scatter on a tray or plate. Lay the butterflied trout fillets in the flour and turn to coat each side well.

Return the frying pan to a medium-high heat. Add the oil and remaining butter to the hot pan. Once the butter has melted and is nicely browned, lay the trout fillets in the pan, flesh side down. Fry until browned on one side, around 2 minutes.

Flip the fillets over and continue to cook them for a further 2–3 minutes on the skin side, using a spoon to baste the fish with the nutty butter. Remove the fish to a plate; keep warm.

Halve the hard-boiled eggs and separate the white and yolk. Slice the egg white and grate the yolk.

Place the frying pan back over a medium-high heat. Once hot, return the pine nuts to the pan then pour in the vermouth and let bubble to deglaze and reduce by half. Add the lemon zest and juice, hard-boiled egg (white and yolk), white pepper, marjoram and parsley. Stir together over a gentle heat to warm through for 1 minute.

Transfer the trout fillets to warmed plates, placing them skin side up, and remove the skin from one of the fillets on each plate to expose the lovely pink flesh. Spoon the pine nut dressing across the trout and serve immediately.

MEAT

It's true of every chef that you cook the things you most want to eat, and when you write recipes for the foods you're mad keen on, you have an extra layer of enthusiasm. You just can't help it. And that's me when it comes to meat. I'll never stop finding new things to do with it. Whenever I visit other restaurants, or even other countries, I'm always fascinated to see what other people do with meat. I get properly excited!

For me, there's something particularly special about slow-cooked meat dishes. There's a sort of magic that happens when you add seasoning and heat and let them do their own thing for a few hours... or a lot of hours when it comes to cholent, which is one of my favourite recipes in this chapter. And I love ribs of all kinds too. You can't beat that feeling of gnawing on a really tasty bit of meat, getting stuck in – it brings out the caveman in all of us! If you need any convincing, try the dry-rub beef ribs.

Here, I've tried to take fairly simple dishes and make them extra special. So if you have time, I hope you'll have a go at brining the bird for your weekend roast chicken, as that little bit of added effort yields brilliant results. If it's something faster you're after, try the chicken fried steak, a Texan favourite I hope will catch on here because it's simple and really, really good: steak in a crispy, spicy batter served with creamy gravy spiked with a bit of horseradish. It's the ultimate comfort food.

I like to think that if you master one dish, you can use it in several different ways. For example, once you've cracked the beef and beer loaf, you can use that same mixture to make sausages, meatballs and terrines. I'm really hoping that the recipes in this chapter will encourage you to share my enthusiasm for delicious, versatile meat. I'd like them to become blueprints – starting points for you to create your own family favourites.

WEEKEND ROAST CHICKEN

Everybody loves a roast chicken! The most important thing is to buy the best chicken you can afford: the better the chicken, the better the flavour. It's as simple as that. This is a 'weekend chicken', because you need to start it the day before you want to eat it, but don't let that put you off – the recipe is very easy. When you taste it, you'll agree it's worth a little advance planning. SERVES 4–6

1 large chicken, about 2kg,
   giblets removed
1 unwaxed lemon, quartered
A small bunch of rosemary

For the brine
3.5 litres water
300g salt
150g caster sugar
4 bay leaves
1 tbsp mustard seeds
1 tsp black peppercorns
2 unwaxed lemons, sliced

For the rub
50ml olive oil
3 tbsp maple syrup
2 tsp salt
2 tsp cayenne pepper
2 tsp ground cumin
1 tsp freshly ground
   black pepper

First make the brine. Put all the ingredients except the lemons into a large saucepan. Bring to the boil, stirring to dissolve the salt and sugar. Transfer to a bowl or container that will fit the chicken, add the lemon slices and leave to cool. Once cooled, cover with cling film and refrigerate.

Before you go to bed, place the chicken in the brine, making sure it's fully submerged. Cover with cling film or a lid and place in the fridge. Leave to brine overnight for about 8 hours (no more than 12 hours or the chicken will be too salty).

The next morning, lift the chicken from the brine and pat it dry with plenty of kitchen paper. Place on a rack in a large roasting tin and return to the fridge, uncovered, for another 6–8 hours to dry out the skin (ready to crisp up in the oven).

Take the chicken out of the fridge 30 minutes before cooking. Preheat the oven to 140°C/Fan 120°C/Gas 1. Mix the ingredients for the rub together in a bowl, then smear all over the chicken, to coat evenly. Return the bird to the rack in the roasting tin, breast side up, and put the lemon and rosemary in the cavity.

Roast for 3 hours, basting from time to time. The chicken is cooked when a meat thermometer inserted in the thigh area near the breast (but not touching the bone) registers 70°C, or the juices run clear when the same area is pierced with a skewer. For the last 10 minutes, whack the oven temperature up to 220°C/Fan 200°C/Gas 7 to crisp and brown the skin.

Remove from the oven and stand the bird upright to let the juices in the cavity pour into the tin. Cover loosely with foil and rest in a warm place for 10 minutes or so. Serve the chicken with the 'gravy' created by the juices in the tin, and seasonal vegetables.

JERK CHICKEN

If you know my cooking at all, you'll know I love a bit of heat! This spicy Jamaican classic is a great favourite of mine. I like the way that the allspice brings a real complexity to the dish, with its rich clove, cinnamon and ginger notes. Marinating the chicken brings an amazing depth of flavour. SERVES 4

1 medium-large chicken, about 1.7kg, jointed into 8 pieces

For the marinade
1 large onion, roughly chopped
200g red chillies (about 10–12), roughly chopped (seeds and all)
125g ginger, peeled and roughly chopped
200ml dark soy sauce
200ml white wine vinegar
40g freshly ground black pepper
35g ground allspice
3 tbsp thyme leaves

First make the marinade. Put the onion, chillies and ginger into a food processor and blend to a smooth, fine pulp. Add the soy sauce, wine vinegar, black pepper, allspice and thyme leaves and whiz again to blend in the spices.

Put the chicken pieces into a large bowl or plastic container. Pour over the marinade and, using your hands, massage it all over the chicken pieces, making sure each piece is well coated. Cover with cling film and leave to marinate in the fridge for 24 hours to allow the flavours to develop and intensify.

The next day, remove the chicken from the fridge 30 minutes before cooking. Preheat the oven to 190°C/Fan 170°C/Gas 5. Place a wire rack inside a large, deep roasting tin and pour about 2cm of water into the tin. This will steam the chicken during roasting, making it deliciously tender and succulent.

Remove the chicken pieces from the marinade and place them on the rack. Roast in the oven for 35–40 minutes, until cooked through, basting a couple of times with the juices from the roasting tray and some of the marinade – let the chicken cook for at least 20 minutes after the final basting with the marinade. The chicken is cooked when the juices run clear when pierced in the thickest part with a skewer, or the internal temperature registers 70°C on a meat thermometer.

Preheat the grill to high. Place the chicken pieces under the hot grill for a few minutes until richly glazed and dark brown, even charred in places. (Alternatively, you can refrigerate the cooked chicken then chargrill it on the barbecue later, making sure it's piping hot in the middle before you serve it.)

Once grilled and nicely glazed, leave the chicken pieces to rest in a warm place for 10 minutes before serving. Serve simply, with rice and a nice crisp green salad.

PAN-ROASTED CHICKEN WITH MILK GRAVY

This is such a simple and comforting dish, full of the rich flavours of chicken and mushrooms in a lovely milk gravy. The secret is to cook it gently and slowly to extract the maximum flavour. SERVES 4

1 medium-large chicken, about 1.7kg, jointed into 8 pieces
2 tbsp plain flour
2 tsp flaky sea salt
2 tsp cayenne pepper
Vegetable oil, for cooking
Salt and freshly ground black pepper

For the sauce
100ml sweet white wine
50ml malt vinegar
35g butter
1 beef stock cube
20g dried ceps or porcini, blitzed to a powder in a mini food processor
35g plain flour
500ml whole milk
200g button mushrooms, cleaned and quartered

Have the chicken pieces ready at room temperature. Mix the flour, salt and cayenne pepper together and scatter on a large plate. Dust the chicken pieces in the seasoned flour, coating them evenly and shaking off any excess.

Heat a large, non-stick, high-sided sauté pan (big enough to fit all the chicken pieces) over a medium-low heat and add a thin film of oil. When the oil is hot, add the chicken pieces and fry them slowly, turning frequently and carefully to avoid tearing the skin. It will take about 40–45 minutes for the chicken to cook through and turn golden brown all over.

Once cooked, remove the chicken pieces with a slotted spoon to a plate or tray and keep warm while you make the sauce.

Turn up the heat under the pan to medium-high and deglaze the pan with the wine and vinegar, scraping up any tasty bits from the bottom. Let the liquor bubble until reduced to a syrupy glaze. Add the butter and, when it's melted, crumble in the stock cube and sprinkle on the mushroom powder. Now stir in the flour to make a thick paste. Cook, stirring, for a few minutes to cook out the raw flour taste.

Next, pour in the milk a little at a time, whisking well after each addition. Once it is all incorporated, lower the heat and simmer gently for 5–6 minutes until it starts to thicken. Add the mushrooms to the sauce and poach them gently, stirring occasionally, for about 5 minutes until they are tender.

Return the chicken pieces to the pan and warm through, coating them in the sauce. If the sauce is a little too thick, thin it with a little hot water or milk. Season to taste with salt and pepper. Serve with creamy mash and wilted greens.

MEDITERRANEAN CHICKEN

This easy, one-dish chicken dinner is like the top of a really good pizza – without the dough. It takes just a few minutes to throw together and is really tasty. As the tomatoes break down, they release their juices to make a light, fragrant tomato sauce, and the chicken soaks up the flavours of the other ingredients. SERVES 4

4 chicken supremes (bone in), skinned

600g mixed ripe tomatoes, larger ones roughly chopped, cherry tomatoes left whole

30g black olives, pitted

1 garlic clove, sliced

1 tsp dried oregano

60ml extra virgin olive oil

8 slices of Milano salami, or other well-flavoured salami

1 medium red onion, cut into 8 wedges through the root

2 balls of buffalo mozzarella, about 125g each

1 tbsp fine polenta

Salt and freshly ground black pepper

1 tbsp oregano leaves, to finish

Preheat the oven to 200°C/Fan 180°C/Gas 6.

Lightly season the chicken supremes with salt and pepper and place them in an ovenproof dish, about 25cm square.

Toss the tomatoes, olives, garlic and oregano together in a bowl. Trickle over about two-thirds of the olive oil and toss the tomatoes again to coat.

Tip the dressed tomatoes over the chicken, pushing them down well with a spoon so that everything becomes well mixed together. Lay the salami and onion wedges over the chicken, then tear the mozzarella over the top.

Sprinkle over the polenta and bake for 25–30 minutes, until the chicken is cooked through, the onions are charred around the edges and the cheese is bubbling and melted.

Remove from the oven. Trickle over the rest of the olive oil and scatter over the oregano leaves just before serving.

CHICKEN CASSEROLE

This is one of the easiest but also one of the tastiest chicken casseroles you will ever make – it is a one-pot wonder and a great family treat. Based on the classic French poule au pot, it packs in a whole lot of flavours and textures. If you have any of the lovely stock left over, freeze it to use in soups or sauces later. SERVES 4–6

1 medium chicken, about 1.5kg, giblets removed

2 carrots, each cut into 4 pieces

2 celery sticks (tough strings removed with a vegetable peeler), each cut into 4 pieces

1 small white cabbage, about 350g, quartered

1 leek, trimmed and well washed, cut into 6 pieces

½ celeriac, peeled and cut into 4 pieces

8 pickling onions or small shallots, peeled and halved

8 garlic cloves, peeled but left whole

1 cured garlic sausage, about 200g, cut into 1cm dice

100g smoked lardons

½ bunch of thyme

½ bunch of rosemary

1 tsp fennel seeds

1 tsp black peppercorns

1 star anise

700ml chicken stock

Salt and freshly ground black pepper

Preheat the oven to 170°C/Fan 150°C/Gas 3½.

Season the chicken cavity lightly with salt. Put all of the vegetables and the garlic into a large bowl and season with salt and pepper. Toss to mix.

Scatter a layer of vegetables in the bottom of a large, heavy-based flameproof casserole and place the chicken on top. Pack the remaining vegetables, garlic sausage and lardons around the chicken and tuck the thyme, rosemary, fennel seeds, peppercorns and star anise into the pot too.

Pour in the chicken stock. Put the casserole over a medium-high heat and bring to the boil. Cover with a tight-fitting lid. Place in the oven and cook for 1½ hours. Remove from the oven and leave, covered, to rest for 20–30 minutes.

Carefully lift the chicken from the pot onto a baking tray. Use a cook's blowtorch, if you have one, to colour the skin until it's golden. (This isn't essential but it will add colour to the dish.)

Shred the chicken into large pieces and divide it and the vegetables between warmed deep plates. Ladle over some of the broth and pour the rest into a warmed jug to pass around the table.

PULLED DUCK BUNS WITH PLUM SAUCE

I can't get enough of this duck version of pulled pork, with its rich plum sauce. The beauty of duck – like pork – is that it has a great meat-to-fat ratio and really soaks up complex flavours. One of the benefits of this recipe it that you can make it a day or two ahead and then reheat it to serve. SERVES 6

1 large duck, about 2.5kg
4 star anise
1 tbsp Szechuan peppercorns
1 tbsp coriander seeds
1 tbsp flaky sea salt
1 tsp ground ginger

For the plum sauce
1 onion, finely diced
3 garlic cloves, finely grated
100g caster sugar
100ml red wine vinegar
50ml beef stock
150ml dark soy sauce
400g plums, halved and
    stoned
3cm piece of ginger, finely
    grated
Finely grated zest and juice
    of 2 unwaxed limes
2 tbsp clear honey
A dash of Tabasco sauce
Salt and freshly ground
    black pepper

To serve
Steamed buns, pancakes or
    wraps, warmed
1 red chilli, sliced
¼ cucumber, sliced
4 spring onions, trimmed
    and finely shredded

First prepare the duck. Using a sharp knife, carefully score the duck skin all over, making sure you don't go so deep that you cut into the meat. Set aside.

Lightly toast the star anise, Szechuan peppercorns, coriander seeds and salt in a small, dry frying pan over a medium heat, until aromatic. Remove from the pan and let cool slightly then grind to a powder using an electric spice grinder or pestle and mortar. Stir in the ground ginger.

Rub the spice mixture all over the duck, using your hands to massage it into the skin and making sure the duck is well coated all over. Leave to stand for an hour or so, to allow the flavours to develop. (Or leave in the fridge overnight, taking it out an hour before cooking to bring back to room temperature.)

Preheat the oven to 150°C/Fan 130°C/Gas 2. Place the duck, breast side up, on a wire rack inside a large roasting tray and roast for 2½ hours, basting from time to time.

Remove the duck from the oven. Leave until cool enough to handle then carefully pull the skin away from the flesh. Roughly chop the skin into bite-sized pieces. Warm a large, non-stick frying pan over a medium heat and fry the duck skin for a few minutes on each side until it's beautifully crisp. Remove with a slotted spoon to a plate and set aside until you're ready to serve. Reserve some of the fat in the pan.

While the duck is resting, make the sauce. Return the pan with the reserved duck fat to a medium heat. Add the onion and garlic and sauté for about 10 minutes, until softened.

Meanwhile, tip the sugar into a deep-sided pan and warm over a low heat for a few minutes, swirling the pan to melt the sugar evenly. Increase the heat and allow the melted sugar to almost bubble. Watch it carefully as it turns golden at the edges and continue to cook to a rich, golden caramel colour.

Immediately and carefully pour in the wine vinegar, beef stock and soy sauce. As you do so, the caramel will seize a bit, but as it heats, it will melt, creating a smooth, sweet-sour sauce. Bring to the boil, stirring to combine. Add the cooked onion and garlic, plums and ginger. Lower the heat and simmer very gently for about an hour until the sauce has thickened and the plums are softened. Don't let it catch on the bottom of the pan.

Stir in the lime zest and juice, then the honey and finally the Tabasco sauce to taste. Take off the heat and cool slightly, then tip into a jug blender or food processor and whiz until smooth, adding a splash of water to loosen slightly if needed. Pass the sauce through a fine sieve into a clean pan and warm gently.

Shred the duck by flaking the meat away from the bone, using a couple of forks to help pull the meat away. Keep the meat quite chunky, as you want some texture, and try not to leave any behind on the carcass. Put the meat into a bowl.

Add some of the plum sauce to the shredded duck, turning to make sure it's well coated. Check the seasoning, adding a little salt and pepper if you think it needs it.

To serve, pile the shredded duck into steamed buns or onto warm wraps or pancakes and spoon on the plum sauce. Top with sliced chilli, cucumber and spring onions and sprinkle on the crispy fried duck skin. Delicious!

If you have any leftover sauce, refrigerate in a sealed jar for another time – it will be good for up to 10 days.

Illustrated overleaf

TEA-BRINED ROAST DUCK WITH SZECHUAN PEPPER

Tea and duck have a particularly good affinity. In this unusual recipe, steeping the duck in a tea-infused brine first helps to tenderise it and give it a depth of flavour, while the Chinese seasoning ingredients work beautifully with the rich duck meat.
SERVES 4

1 large duck, about 2.5kg

For the brine
2 litres water
75g loose-leaf Earl Grey tea
1 large piece of ginger, about
    60g, roughly chopped
1 head of garlic, halved
    across the middle
100g salt
10 star anise

For the rub
2 tbsp Szechuan peppercorns
1 tbsp flaky sea salt
2 star anise
2 tsp ground ginger
2 tsp smoked paprika

For the glaze
100g clear honey
150ml dark soy sauce

First prepare the brine. Put the water, tea, ginger, garlic, salt and star anise into a large saucepan and bring to the boil, stirring to dissolve the salt. Remove from the heat and set aside to cool.

Pour the cooled brine through a fine sieve into a container large enough to fit the duck snugly. Lower the duck into the brine, making sure it's submerged, then cover with cling film. Refrigerate for 12 hours.

Remove the duck from the fridge, lift it out of the brine and pat dry with kitchen paper – you might want to do this over the sink. Set aside while you prepare the rub.

Preheat the oven to 140°C/Fan 120°C/Gas 1.

For the rub, heat a small, dry frying pan over a medium heat and add the Szechuan peppercorns, flaky sea salt and star anise. Toast in the pan, shaking occasionally, for 2–3 minutes until lightly golden and aromatic. Remove from the pan and leave to cool slightly.

Using an electric spice grinder or pestle and mortar, grind the toasted mix to a powder then pass through a sieve to remove the coarser bits. Tip the powdered spice mix into a small bowl and stir in the ground ginger and smoked paprika.

Rub the spice mixture all over the duck, using your hands to thoroughly massage it into the skin. Sit the duck, breast side up, on a wire rack placed in a large roasting tray. Roast in the oven for 2½ hours, basting from time to time.

While the duck is cooking, make the glaze. Pour the honey into a medium saucepan and warm over a gentle heat until it turns to a rich amber caramel. Carefully pour in the soy sauce and mix together. Remove from the heat.

Remove the duck from the oven and turn the oven setting up to 220°C/Fan 200°C/Gas 7. Using a pastry brush, baste the honey and soy glaze all over the duck.

Return the glazed duck to the oven and roast for a further 15–20 minutes, basting and brushing with the honey and soy glaze every 5–8 minutes. After this time, the duck will be lovely and moist and a dark, golden brown. Remove the duck from the oven and let it rest in a warm place for 20 minutes, covered lightly with foil.

Transfer the duck to a serving platter and serve with wilted bok choi and some steamed jasmine rice.

SPICED ROAST RUMP OF LAMB WITH CELERY & FETA

I love the flavour of a rump of lamb. It's such a good cut of meat but you do have to use your teeth, and the fact that you need to chew it helps release all of those amazing flavours. The clean, almost botanical taste of the celery acts as an excellent counterbalance to the rich, succulent lamb. SERVES 2

2 rumps of lamb, about 250g each
Vegetable oil, for cooking

For the rub
2 tsp fennel seeds
½ tsp cloves
½ tsp black peppercorns
2 tsp English mustard powder
2 garlic cloves, finely grated
1 tsp dried thyme
1 tsp dried rosemary
Flaky sea salt and freshly ground black pepper

For the celery
½ head of celery (about 200g), trimmed
2–3 tbsp good extra virgin olive oil
1 onion, finely diced
2 red chillies, sliced into rings (seeds removed for less heat, if preferred)
½–1 tbsp yellow mustard seeds, to taste (more or less heat)
1 tbsp red wine vinegar
2 tbsp chopped dill
80g feta cheese, cubed

Preheat the oven to 180°C/Fan 160°C/Gas 4.

First make the rub for the lamb. Warm a small, dry frying pan over a gentle heat and add the fennel seeds, cloves and peppercorns. Heat for 2–3 minutes, shaking the pan from time to time, until the seeds are evenly toasted and aromatic. Let cool slightly, then grind to a fine powder using an electric spice grinder or pestle and mortar.

Tip the ground spices into a small bowl and add the mustard powder, garlic, thyme and rosemary and a good sprinkling of salt. Stir well to combine.

Sprinkle the spice rub onto the lamb rumps and massage into the meat with your hands, to coat thoroughly all over.

Drizzle a little oil into a large, ovenproof, non-stick frying pan and place over a high heat. Once it's hot, add the lamb rumps and cook for about 8 minutes, turning frequently, so they're nicely seared and have taken on plenty of colour. They should be evenly caramelised all over.

Transfer the frying pan to the oven and roast the rumps for 5–6 minutes for medium-rare, allowing a couple of minutes longer if you prefer your lamb cooked medium. Remove from the oven, lift the lamb onto a tray or plate, and leave to rest in a warm place, covered lightly with foil.

While the lamb is in the oven, prepare the celery. Remove the tough strings with a vegetable peeler, then slice on the diagonal into 1cm pieces.

Heat a non-stick frying pan over a medium heat and add
2 tbsp olive oil. Add the onion and sauté for about 10 minutes
until softened, stirring from time to time. Add the celery slices,
chillies and mustard seeds and continue to cook for about
5 minutes, until the celery is just softened.

Add any juices from the pan the lamb was cooked in. If it
looks a little dry, add a splash more oil or water. Mix in the
wine vinegar and chopped dill and season to taste with salt
and pepper. Warm through for a minute or two, then stir in
the feta cheese and remove from the heat.

Slice the lamb rumps thickly and arrange on warmed plates
with the celery and feta alongside.

SLOW-ROASTED LAMB WITH HOT FENNEL RELISH

Lamb is such a versatile meat, it can handle bold flavours exceptionally well. In this recipe, toasted fennel seeds give the lamb shoulder a wonderful, aniseed-y crust. Roasting the joint on a 'trivet' of fennel and onion wedges, which is then transformed into a fantastic warm relish, makes even more of this classic and delicious pairing.

SERVES 6–8

1 shoulder of lamb, bone in, about 2–2.2kg

For the rub
4 tbsp fennel seeds
1 tbsp black peppercorns
1 tbsp flaky sea salt
3 tbsp Dijon mustard

For roasting
3 fennel bulbs, quartered
2 onions, quartered
125ml white wine
75ml olive oil

For the relish
3 tbsp white wine vinegar
2 green chillies, chopped (seeds and all)
A small bunch of dill, chopped
½ bunch of mint, tough stalks removed, leaves chopped
Salt and freshly ground black pepper

For the sauce
150ml lamb or beef stock

Preheat the oven to 150°C/Fan 130°C/Gas 2.

Place the lamb shoulder on a board and, using a sharp knife, score the skin all over, making sure you don't go so deep that you cut into the flesh. Set aside while you prepare the rub.

Warm a small, dry frying pan over a medium heat and add the fennel seeds, peppercorns and sea salt. Heat for 2–3 minutes, shaking the pan from time to time, until the seeds are lightly toasted and aromatic. Remove from the pan and let cool slightly, then grind coarsely using an electric spice grinder or pestle and mortar.

Brush the mustard all over the surface of the lamb on both sides, to coat the meat evenly and generously. Sprinkle the fennel seed mixture on top of this, rubbing and patting it into the mustard coating with your hands.

Put the fennel and onion quarters into a large roasting tray, to cover the base. Pour in the white wine. Sit the lamb on top and drizzle over the olive oil. Roast for 4–5 hours, basting from time to time, until the meat is very tender and falling off the bone.

Transfer the lamb to a large plate, cover loosely with foil and leave to rest in a warm place while you make the relish.

For the relish, remove the fennel and onion from the roasting tray and place on a board. Roughly chop to a 'salsa' texture and place in a bowl with the wine vinegar, chillies and herbs. Give it a good stir and season to taste with salt and pepper.

Place the roasting tray containing all the lovely lamb juices over a high heat on the hob. Once the juices start to bubble away, pour in the stock to deglaze. Let bubble for 5–10 minutes or until reduced and thickened, whisking frequently. Strain through a sieve into a warmed jug.

Serve the lamb whole or flaked into pieces, with the hot fennel relish and sauce. I find this goes brilliantly with potato salad or pitta breads.

MARINATED LAMB RIBS WITH ROASTED ONIONS

Lamb 'ribs' are actually the breast of lamb, a cut which needs slow cooking to enjoy it at its tender best. Allow 3 to 4 hours' marinating before cooking them too, to get as much flavour as possible going on. This is a great dish to cook in the oven and then finish on the barbecue for an extra whack of flavour. SERVES 4–6

1 breast of lamb, bones in, about 1.5kg
6 onions, peeled with the root left on
10 garlic cloves, peeled
1 tbsp thyme leaves

For the marinade
4 tbsp black treacle
4 tbsp malt vinegar
2 tbsp soft light brown sugar
1 tbsp dried oregano
2 tsp salt
1 tsp smoked paprika
1 unwaxed lemon

For the purée and glaze
2 tbsp chopped salted anchovies
5 tbsp chopped mint leaves
1 tbsp malt vinegar
1 unwaxed lemon
Salt and freshly ground black pepper

First prepare the marinade. In a small bowl, mix together the treacle, malt vinegar, brown sugar, oregano, salt and smoked paprika to combine. Finely grate in the zest of the lemon and stir together.

Place the lamb breast in a suitable plastic container or on a large platter. Pour the marinade over the lamb and use your hands to massage it in so it completely coats the ribs. Cover with a lid or cling film and leave to marinate in the fridge for 3–4 hours to allow the flavours to develop.

Preheat the oven to 150°C/Fan 130°C/Gas 2.

Line the base of a large roasting tin with foil. Quarter the onions vertically, through the root. Place the onion quarters and garlic cloves in the roasting tray and scatter over the thyme leaves. Cut the zested lemon (used for the marinade) in half and snuggle this in among the onions. Sit the lamb breast on top.

Lay a large second sheet of foil over the top of the lamb and scrunch the edges of the foil together to form a tightly sealed parcel, which encases the lamb. Be careful to make sure there aren't any holes for the steam to escape. Roast in the oven for 4 hours.

Remove the lamb from the oven and leave it to rest in its foil parcel for 15 minutes. Open the foil and carefully remove the lamb. It should be lovely and tender and falling away from the bone. Set the ribs aside and keep warm while you prepare the onions for the purée and glaze.

Remove the cooked onions and garlic from the roasting tin and place in a bowl. Using a fork, crush them to a rough purée; it should be soft but still with a little texture. Stir through the chopped anchovies, mint and malt vinegar, then season to taste with salt and pepper. Set the roasted onion purée aside.

To make the glaze, strain the lamb cooking juices from the roasting tin through a sieve into a saucepan and place over a medium heat. Bring to the boil and let bubble to reduce and thicken for a few minutes to create a sticky glaze.

Grate the zest of the lemon over the ribs and transfer to a serving board or platter; the lemon will cut through the rich flavours and add an extra acidity and tangy flavour. Finally, coat the lamb ribs with the sticky glaze.

Cut the lamb into chunks. Serve with the roasted onion purée alongside, with some of the pan juices trickled over the top.

CHICKEN FRIED STEAK

I'm really fond of this simple Texan dish. Bashed-out sirloin steak is dredged in a spicy coating and fried until crisp, then served with a rich, creamy gravy. Just add mash and some buttery green beans for the ultimate comfort food... SERVES 2–4

2 sirloin steaks, about
    250g each and 1.5cm
    thick, trimmed of all fat
2 eggs
½ tsp cayenne pepper
Vegetable oil, for cooking

For the spice mix
4 tbsp plain flour
2 tsp salt
1 tsp garlic powder
1 tsp smoked paprika
½ tsp ground cumin
½ tsp ground cinnamon
½ tsp freshly ground
    black pepper
½ tsp dried thyme

For the sauce
1 tbsp plain flour
1 chicken stock cube
275ml whole milk
1 tbsp thyme leaves
1 tbsp freshly grated
    horseradish
Lemon juice, to taste
Salt and freshly ground
    black pepper

To garnish
Soft thyme leaves
Flaky sea salt

Lay a sheet of cling film on a board, place the steaks on top and cover with a second sheet of cling film. Using a rolling pin or meat mallet, bash out the steaks until they're half their original thickness. Cut each piece in half, so you have 4 pieces.

In a bowl, beat the eggs with the cayenne pepper. For the spice mix, in a separate bowl, mix the flour, salt, garlic powder, spices, pepper and thyme together.

One by one, dip each steak into the egg, then into the spice mixture, to coat generously. Dip back into the egg, shaking off any excess, then back into the spice mix.

Warm a glug of oil in a medium non-stick frying pan over a medium-high heat. Once hot, add two of the steak pieces and fry until golden brown and crispy. This will take about 1½ minutes per side for medium-rare. Allow an extra minute for medium, but don't cook for too long, or they won't crisp up. Transfer the cooked steaks to a warmed plate and keep warm while you cook the other two. Let them all rest for 5 minutes.

Meanwhile, make the sauce. Pour off any excess fat, keeping around 1 tbsp juices in the pan. Return to the heat, add the flour and whisk constantly until it is nicely browned, as this will give the gravy a great flavour. Crumble in the chicken stock cube and once it's dissolved, gradually pour in the milk, whisking all the time to keep the sauce smooth.

Lower the heat and simmer gently for 4–5 minutes until thickened. Season to taste with salt and pepper, stir through the thyme and horseradish, and finish with a squeeze of lemon juice to sharpen the flavour.

Spoon the gravy onto warmed plates and arrange the chicken fried steaks on top. Scatter with thyme and a little flaky sea salt and serve at once.

DRY-RUB BEEF RIBS

Slow cooking short ribs is the only way to go – the connective tissue breaks down, giving way to a juicy and tender piece of beef which is addictively delicious. The spicy, herby dry rub adds great flavour and the sticky dark glaze helps to create a crust. This is the perfect thing to tuck into on a hot day, with a few cold beers.

SERVES 6

2.2kg short ribs of beef
on the bone
6 tbsp prepared English
mustard

For the rub
2 tbsp flaky sea salt
1 tbsp smoked paprika
1 tbsp garlic powder
1 tbsp celery salt
1 tbsp dried thyme
1 tbsp dried sage
½ tbsp freshly ground
black pepper
½ tbsp chilli powder

For the glaze
100ml apple juice
2 tbsp golden syrup
2 tbsp black treacle
2 tbsp clear honey
2 tbsp Worcestershire sauce
1 beef stock cube

Preheat the oven to 140°C/Fan 120°C/Gas 1.

First prepare the rub. Place all of the ingredients in a small bowl and stir to combine.

Using a pastry brush or spoon, smear the mustard all over the short ribs, to coat them generously. Scatter the dry rub over the mustard and use your hands to pat it on evenly.

Place the pieces of meat in a large roasting tin then roast, uncovered, for 5 hours, basting several times during cooking with the juices in the tin.

When the roasting time is almost up, prepare the glaze. Place the apple juice, golden syrup, black treacle, honey and Worcestershire sauce in a bowl and crumble in the stock cube. Whisk to combine.

Remove the roasting tin from the oven and pour the glaze all over the beef. Return to the oven and roast for a further 45 minutes, basting every 10–15 minutes with the juices.

Now turn the oven up to 160°C/Fan 140°C/Gas 3. Roast the beef for a final 30–40 minutes, until it's deep golden brown and the glaze is deliciously sticky. The beef will be very tender, falling off the bone and juicy.

Remove from the oven, brush with the cooking juices and leave to rest in a warm place for 20–30 minutes, covered lightly with foil.

Carve the beef into generous slices and serve with the cooking juices spooned over.

BEEF & BEER LOAF

Beef and beer go so well together – it's one of the great combinations – and they're fantastic in this tasty version of meatloaf. In a final flourish, I blowtorch the surface right at the end to give it a distinctive charred and toasty flavour. You could also use this mixture to make beef sausages, or even serve it as a cold beef terrine, with mustard and pickles. SERVES 8

Vegetable oil, for cooking
1 large onion, diced
450g coarsely minced beef brisket, chilled
450g coarsely minced beef rump, chilled
180g coarsely minced beef fat, chilled
140g fresh breadcrumbs
140ml strong ale, chilled
3 garlic cloves, finely grated
1 tbsp malt extract
1 tbsp prepared English mustard
1 tbsp thyme leaves
1 tbsp flaky sea salt
1 tsp soft light brown sugar
1 tsp cracked black pepper
1 tsp cayenne pepper

For the glaze
1½ tbsp black treacle
1 tbsp prepared English mustard
1 tbsp beef stock
½ tbsp red wine vinegar

To garnish
1 tbsp soft thyme leaves

Heat a glug of oil in a medium, non-stick frying pan over a medium-low heat and add the onion. Cook gently, stirring from time to time, for around 10–15 minutes until soft and translucent. Remove from the heat and allow to cool.

Put all the chilled minced beef and beef fat into a large bowl. Add the cooled onion, breadcrumbs, ale, garlic, malt extract, mustard, thyme, salt, sugar, pepper and cayenne. Using your hands, mix thoroughly until well combined and starting to firm up – this may take 5 minutes or so. The more you work it, the better it will hold together on cooking.

Lay a large rectangle of foil on a flat surface. Trickle a little oil into the centre and rub it all over the foil – this will prevent the loaf sticking during cooking.

Place the beef mixture in the middle of the foil and spread it out to create a sausage shape that will fit into a 1kg loaf tin. Make sure you form the mixture very tightly so that it has no air pockets. Use the foil to help you roll up the beef 'sausage', ensuring it's packed tightly and completely encased. Wrap in two more layers of foil. Secure the ends by scrunching them up tightly.

Place the wrapped beef loaf in the fridge and leave it to rest and firm up for at least 1 hour, or overnight if that's more convenient for you.

When you're ready to cook the loaf, preheat the oven to 180°C/ Fan 160°C/Gas 4. Place the foil-wrapped loaf in a 1kg loaf tin, pressing it in tightly so the meat mixture goes right into the corners. (Alternatively, simply place the foil-wrapped 'sausage' in a roasting tin.) Roast for about 1 hour.

Meanwhile, prepare the glaze. Put all the ingredients into a small saucepan and bring to the boil over a medium-high heat. Lower the heat slightly and simmer to reduce until thickened to a sticky glaze. Remove from the heat; keep warm.

To test whether the loaf is cooked, insert a meat thermometer into the centre; it should register an internal temperature of at least 70°C. It may need an extra 5 minutes or so.

Once cooked, set aside in a warm place to rest for 10 minutes, then carefully remove the foil. Use a cook's blowtorch to give the loaf a blast so it's nicely charred and has a lovely shiny deep brown colour all over. If you don't have a blowtorch, you could flash the loaf under a hot grill for a minute or two.

Brush the beef loaf with the glaze and scatter over the thyme leaves. Serve carved into thick slices, with some creamy mash on the side if you like.

CHOLENT

This classic Jewish dish of beef, beans and barley is the ultimate slow-cooked beef, taking 12–15 hours! It evolved from the religious law prohibiting the lighting of fires on the Sabbath. Traditionally, the pot was brought to the boil before dusk on Friday then left to simmer away so there would be a hot meal the following day. You can cook it all day or overnight and it reheats beautifully. Filling, warming and full of flavour, it's a wonderful family dish. SERVES 6–8

Vegetable oil, for cooking

1.2kg stewing beef, short rib or brisket, cut into large pieces

8 carrots, halved

8–10 small turnips, peeled and halved

2 large onions, diced, skins reserved

15 garlic cloves, finely grated

3 tbsp clear honey

1 tbsp smoked paprika

1 tbsp salt

2 tsp cracked black pepper

200g dried butter beans, soaked in water for 1 hour then drained

100g pearl barley

A small bunch of rosemary, tied with kitchen string

About 1.5 litres water

Preheat the oven to 120°C/Fan 100°C/Gas ½.

Heat a glug of oil in a large, heavy-based flameproof casserole (that has a tight-fitting lid) over a high heat. Brown the beef well in batches all over; you want it to take on plenty of colour, so don't overcrowd the pan. Once browned, remove from the pan with a slotted spoon and set aside while you colour the rest of the beef, adding a little more oil to the pan if necessary.

Add the carrots to the pan and sauté until well caramelised all over and sticky. You want to add plenty of colour and flavour to the vegetables. Remove the carrots from the pan and set aside with the beef. Sauté the turnips in the pan, in the same way, then remove and set aside.

Reduce the heat to medium-low and add the onions and garlic to the pan. Cook, turning frequently, for around 8–10 minutes until they are softened and well coloured. Stir in the honey, paprika, salt and pepper and cook for 1 minute.

Return the beef and browned vegetables to the pan and stir well. Add the butter beans, pearl barley and rosemary, and give it all a good stir again. Pour in just enough water to cover the meat, then increase the heat and bring to the boil. Add the onion skins (these lend colour). Put the lid on the casserole and cook in the oven for 12–15 hours.

Check on the cholent a couple of times during cooking, giving it a stir and topping up the liquid if necessary with boiling water from the kettle so the meat is just covered. By the end of cooking, the meat should be very tender and falling apart. Take out the rosemary and onion skins. Serve the cholent ladled into warmed bowls.

MEATBALLS IN CHUNKY TREACLE GRAVY

These meatballs are so easy to make and full of rich flavours – everyone loves them! Finished off with a dark and delicious gravy, the humble meatball is taken to a whole new level. They're even better the next day, too. Serve with spaghetti or simple boiled rice and a scattering of grated full-flavoured Cheddar if you like, or just let the full-on flavour of the treacle gravy do the work. SERVES 6–8

Vegetable oil, for cooking
2 onions, finely diced
1.2kg minced beef or pork
80g dry breadcrumbs
3 tbsp Dijon mustard
1 tbsp cracked black pepper
1 tsp dried oregano
1 tsp dried sage
1 tsp ground allspice
2 tsp salt
2 eggs, lightly beaten

For the gravy
2 red onions, diced
2 red peppers, cored,
    deseeded and diced
2 red chillies, diced (seeds
    and all if you like the
    heat)
8 garlic cloves, finely grated
100ml malt vinegar
1 tbsp brown sugar
50g black treacle
75ml Worcestershire sauce
1 tbsp Dijon mustard
½ tsp smoked paprika
600ml beef stock
100ml stout
4 tomatoes
Salt and freshly ground
    black pepper

Heat a splash of oil in a non-stick frying pan over a medium-low heat and add the onions. Fry for around 10 minutes, stirring from time to time, until softened. Leave to cool.

Transfer the cooled onions to a large bowl and add the mince, breadcrumbs, mustard, pepper, oregano, sage, allspice, salt and eggs. Mix together, using your hands, until thoroughly combined. The more you work the mixture, the better the meatballs will hold together on cooking. Cover the bowl with cling film and chill for at least an hour, or overnight.

Divide the mixture into 16–20 even-sized pieces. Form into balls and roll each one between your hands to shape neatly. Place the balls on a plate or tray, cover with cling film and refrigerate for a further 30 minutes. Chilling the meatballs helps prevent them breaking up during cooking.

Preheat the oven to 190°C/Fan 170°C/Gas 5.

Remove the meatballs from the fridge, place them in a roasting tray and roast in the oven for 25 minutes.

While the meatballs are cooking, make the gravy. Heat a splash of oil in a large, non-stick, deep sauté pan over a medium-low heat. Add the onions, peppers, chillies and garlic and fry for 10 minutes, stirring from time to time, until softened.

Turn up the heat, pour in the malt vinegar and add the sugar, stirring to deglaze and dissolve the sugar. Simmer until the mixture is well reduced to a sticky glaze.

Stir in the treacle, Worcestershire sauce, mustard and paprika. Pour in the beef stock and stout and bring to the boil over a high heat. Lower the heat and simmer gently until the gravy is reduced by about a third.

Meanwhile, skin the tomatoes (see page 14) and roughly chop them. Once the meatballs are cooked, remove them from the oven and set aside.

Add the meatballs and chopped tomatoes to the reduced gravy. Give it a stir, being careful not to bash the meatballs, and continue to simmer gently over a low heat for a further 10 minutes, until the sauce has reduced slightly. Taste and adjust the seasoning with salt and pepper if necessary. Remove from the heat.

Serve the meatballs with the rich treacle gravy spooned over.

DEEP-PAN MEAT FEAST PIZZA

Thin-crust pizzas might be more fashionable now, but there's something really satisfying about a deep-pan pizza if it's done well. Get a great dough and a zingy tomato sauce working together, and you've got the perfect base to build on – you can really give your imagination free rein. This recipe makes more tomato sauce than you'll need here, but it keeps well in the fridge for a few days and you can use it for your next batch of pizzas, or as a sauce for pasta. SERVES 2

For the dough
750g '00' flour, plus extra
    for dusting
2 tbsp olive oil, plus extra
    for oiling
1 tbsp caster sugar
2 tsp salt
7g sachet fast-action dried
    yeast
60ml warm milk
375ml warm water

For the tomato sauce
400g tin chopped tomatoes
2 tbsp tomato purée
4 tsp white wine vinegar
1 tbsp soft light brown sugar
½ tbsp dried oregano
2 garlic cloves, finely grated
Salt and freshly ground
    black pepper

For the beef layer
250g minced beef
1 tsp fennel seeds
1 tbsp thyme leaves
1 garlic clove, finely grated

To make the dough, put all the ingredients into a freestanding mixer with the dough hook fitted and mix until combined. Continue to knead in the mixer for about 10 minutes, until the dough is smooth, silky and elastic. You may need to add an extra 1 tbsp water if the dough feels a little tight.

Transfer the dough to a lightly oiled large bowl and cover with cling film. Leave to rise in a warm place until it's doubled in size – this should take about an hour or so.

While the dough is rising, make the tomato sauce. Put the tomatoes, tomato purée, wine vinegar, sugar, oregano and garlic in a medium saucepan. Give it a good stir and bring to the boil over a medium-high heat. Lower the heat and simmer, stirring from time to time, until the sauce is reduced by half. Season to taste with salt and pepper, take off the heat and set aside to cool completely.

Meanwhile, prepare the beef layer. Place a medium, non-stick frying pan over a high heat. When hot, add the mince and dry-fry for 10–15 minutes, stirring frequently, until dry, brown and crispy. Using a slotted spoon, remove the mince from the pan, drain off any excess fat and transfer to a bowl.

Wipe out the frying pan with kitchen paper and return it to a medium-high heat. Add the fennel seeds and rattle them around in the pan for a couple of minutes until fragrant and toasted. Add them to the mince along with the thyme leaves and garlic. Season to taste with salt and pepper and let cool.

For the topping
150g sliced garlic sausage
2 small red onions, thinly
    sliced
2 small red chillies, sliced
    (seeds and all, if you like
    the heat)
10 thin slices of pancetta
2 balls of buffalo mozzarella,
    about 125g each
50g Parmesan cheese,
    freshly grated

To finish
A bunch of basil, leaves
    picked from the stems

Preheat the oven to 200°C/Fan 180°C/Gas 6. Lightly oil two 30cm deep-sided, non-stick ovenproof frying pans, or a shallow rectangular oven tray, about 32 x 42cm and 7cm deep. Wipe away any excess oil with kitchen paper.

Once the dough has risen, turn it out onto a lightly floured surface, knock back and knead for a couple of minutes.

If you're using two pans, divide the dough in half and use a floured rolling pin to roll each portion into a round, about 1cm thick. Alternatively, roll the dough into a rectangle to fit the oven tray. Push the pizza dough into each pan, or the tray, pressing it up the edges and moulding it with your hands to fit the base and sides.

Spread a layer of tomato sauce over each pizza (about 4–6 tbsp for the round pizzas, 6–8 tbsp for the rectangular one), using a spoon or spatula to distribute it evenly. Don't overdo it or the dough will become soggy (keep any excess tomato sauce for another occasion).

Scatter the fried minced beef evenly over each pizza and arrange the slices of garlic sausage on top. Add the onion and chilli slices, then the pancetta. Tear the mozzarella balls into pieces and arrange evenly over the pizza(s). Finally, sprinkle on the Parmesan cheese and you're ready to go!

Bake for 25–30 minutes, until the pancetta is cooked, the cheese is melted and bubbling, and the edges of the dough are lovely and crisp.

Remove the pizza(s) from the oven and allow to stand for a few minutes before scattering over the basil leaves. Remove the pizza(s) from the pan and cut into wedges. Serve at once.

Illustrated overleaf

OX CHEEKS WITH HORSERADISH

Ox cheeks are full of flavour and have an amazing unctious, melting texture when cooked slowly. In this recipe, I gently steam the meat in some stock and stout, which gives it a real depth of rich, dark tastes. The zingy noisette dressing cuts through the richness of the ox cheeks. To give it an extra layer, I include some smoked butter but if you can't find it, simply up the quantity of ordinary butter – there are so many great flavours in this dish, it'll still be fantastic. SERVES 4

4 ox cheeks, about 400g
    each, trimmed of sinew
Vegetable oil, for cooking
3 banana shallots, thinly
    sliced, skins reserved
3 garlic cloves, finely grated
350ml beef stock
250ml stout
A small bunch of thyme
2 tbsp malt vinegar
2 tsp black treacle
A piece of fresh horseradish,
    about 5cm long, peeled
Salt and freshly ground
    black pepper

For the rub
2 tbsp English mustard
    powder
2 tbsp flaky sea salt
2 tbsp soft light brown sugar
1 tbsp hot smoked paprika
1 tbsp cracked black pepper

First prepare the rub. Put all the ingredients into a small bowl and stir to combine.

Place the ox cheeks in a plastic container or on a large plate and dredge the rub evenly over the cheeks, using your hands to massage it in and ensure they are well coated. Cover with cling film and refrigerate for 4–8 hours to allow the flavours to develop and intensify.

Preheat the oven to 140°C/Fan 120°C/Gas 1.

Heat a glug of oil in a large, heavy-based flameproof casserole over a high heat. Season the ox cheeks with salt and pepper and sear them in the pan for a few minutes on each side, until they are dark all over. Remove from the pan and set aside.

Reduce the heat under the pan to medium-low and add the sliced shallots and garlic. Cook for 8–10 minutes, stirring frequently, until they are softened and have taken on some colour. Meanwhile, tie the thyme sprigs and shallot skins into bundles with kitchen string. Pour the beef stock and stout into the casserole and bring to the boil.

Once the stock is bubbling, add the ox cheeks and drop the thyme and shallot skin bundles into the pan. Put the lid on and transfer the casserole to the oven to braise for 4 hours.

Remove the pan from the oven and lift out the ox cheeks. Set aside on a tray or plate, cover with foil and keep warm.

For the noisette dressing
75g butter
20g smoked butter
Juice of 1 lime
3 tbsp chopped pitted dates
2 tbsp capers

Return the pan to a high heat and allow the sauce to bubble until thickened and reduced to a rich glaze. Pass the sauce through a fine sieve into a clean, large pan and stir in the malt vinegar and treacle. Heat through.

Return the ox cheeks to the pan. Using a fine grater, grate about 2 tbsp of the horseradish (save a little for the noisette) on top of the cheeks and use a spoon to roll them around in the mixture to absorb all the lovely flavours. Gently warm through.

For the noisette dressing, melt the butter and smoked butter together in a medium saucepan. Heat until it turns a rich, nutty brown, then add the lime juice, dates and capers. Grate in the remaining horseradish, season with salt and pepper and swirl the pan to combine all the flavours. Remove from the heat.

Spoon the ox cheeks and sauce onto warmed plates and trickle over some of the noisette dressing. Serve immediately.

VENISON CHOPS WITH CRANBERRIES & RED WINE

I love venison. It is packed with flavour and makes a tasty alternative to beef. However, you need to take care when frying it, as its very low fat content gives it a tendency to dry out if at all overcooked. Look for thick chops to ensure they stay nice and moist. If you find venison chops hard to track down, this recipe works brilliantly with pork chops too, or even lamb. Cranberries have a great acidity that goes very well with game, and also pork and lamb. I like to serve it with mash to soak up the delicious sauce, but tagliatelle goes well too. SERVES 4

4 large, bone-in venison
  chops, at least 2.5cm
  thick, or 4 bone-in pork
  or lamb loin chops
  (similarly thick)
Sea salt and freshly ground
  black pepper

For the marinade
½ bunch of thyme
6 juniper berries, crushed
2 bay leaves
Zest of ½ unwaxed orange,
  finely pared with a
  vegetable peeler
400ml red wine

For the cranberry sauce
Vegetable oil, for frying
3 banana shallots, finely
  diced
2 large portobello
  mushrooms, finely diced
75g cranberry jelly
Juice of 1 orange
50ml red wine vinegar
200ml beef stock
150g cranberries
30g butter

First marinate the chops. Place them in a plastic container and scatter over the thyme sprigs, juniper berries, bay leaves and orange zest. Pour over the red wine, making sure the chops are fully submerged. Cover with cling film or a lid and leave to marinate in the fridge for at least 3-4 hours, ideally overnight.

Remove the chops from the marinade and set aside. Strain the marinade through a sieve into a jug, and reserve for the sauce.

To make the sauce, heat a splash of oil in a medium, deep sauté pan, or a saucepan, over a medium heat. Add the shallots and mushrooms and cook for about 8-10 minutes, stirring from time to time, until they are softened.

Stir in the cranberry jelly, then pour in the orange juice and wine vinegar and stir to combine. Turn up the heat and let the liquid bubble until most of it has evaporated and the sautéed vegetables are just glazed with the glossy sauce.

Pour in the reserved marinade and the beef stock. Bring to the boil, then turn the heat right down and simmer very gently for around 10-15 minutes, until the sauce is just thick enough to coat the back of a spoon. You may need to skim it from time to time to remove any scum that rises to the surface.

Stir in the cranberries and simmer for 4-5 minutes, or a little longer if you think the sauce needs to reduce down a bit more. Season to taste with salt and pepper.

To finish
Flaky sea salt

While the sauce is on the go, fry the chops. Heat a glug of oil in a large, non-stick frying pan over a high heat. Season the chops with salt and pepper. Once the oil is hot, add the chops and cook until they are nicely coloured and golden brown. Allow 2–3 minutes on each side for medium-rare venison chops. If you're cooking pork chops, allow 5–6 minutes each side. For lamb chops allow 4–5 minutes each side.

Just before the chops are done, add the butter to the pan and, once melted, use it to baste the meat. Remove the pan from the heat and transfer the chops to a warmed plate. Leave to rest in a warm place for 5–10 minutes, covered lightly in foil.

Serve the venison chops on warmed plates with the cranberry sauce spooned over and sprinkled with a little flaky sea salt.

VENISON CHILLI

I love a regular beef chilli, but this venison version is something else! Using a combination of diced haunch and venison mince gives the dish a real depth of flavour and a great texture. Although it takes a bit more time, the recipe is pretty straightforward and the result is well worth it. Finishing the rich dish with dark chocolate, red wine and a zing of lime perks it up beautifully. SERVES 6–8

For the venison haunch
Vegetable oil, for cooking
1kg venison haunch, diced
2 carrots, halved
4 celery sticks, cut in half
1 onion, quartered
Bouquet garni (sprig each of
    thyme and rosemary and
    a bay leaf, tied together
    with kitchen string)
2 garlic cloves, sliced
1 litre dark rich beef or
    venison stock

For the chilli
2 tbsp cumin seeds
2 tbsp coriander seeds
2 tsp chilli powder
2 tsp cracked black pepper
400g minced venison
Vegetable oil, for cooking
2 onions, diced
4 garlic cloves, finely grated
150g Milano salami or
    chorizo, diced
400g tin kidney beans,
    drained and rinsed
150ml red wine
Finely grated zest of
    1 unwaxed lime
75g dark chocolate (70%
    cocoa solids), grated
Salt and freshly ground
    black pepper

Preheat the oven to 140°C/Fan 120°C/Gas 1.

Heat a glug of oil in a large, heavy-based flameproof casserole over a high heat. Sear the diced venison, in batches to avoid overcrowding the pan, for a few minutes until well coloured on all sides. Remove with a slotted spoon and set aside in a bowl.

Once all the meat is browned, lower the heat, add the carrots to the pan and sauté until they have taken on plenty of colour. Now add the celery, onion and bouquet garni and fry for a few minutes. Add the garlic and cook for another minute or two.

Return the meat to the casserole, pour in the stock and bring to the boil. Put the lid on and transfer to the oven. Braise for 3 hours until the meat is succulent and deliciously tender.

Remove the meat from the oven and let cool slightly. Place a colander over a bowl. Tip the venison braise into the colander to strain off the stock. Reserve the stock and separate the meat from the vegetables. Transfer the meat to a bowl and set aside. Discard the vegetables and bouquet garni.

For the chilli, place a small frying pan over a medium heat and add the cumin and coriander seeds. Toast for 2–3 minutes, rattling the pan, until fragrant. Let cool slightly, then grind to a powder using an electric spice grinder or pestle and mortar. Tip into a bowl and mix in the chilli powder and black pepper.

Heat a large, non-stick frying pan over a medium heat. Add the minced venison and dry-fry for about 20–25 minutes, stirring frequently, until the mince is nicely browned and has a tasty, nutty flavour. It should be very crispy. Drain the mince in a colander to remove any excess fat and set aside.

To serve
Crème fraîche
A few gratings of dark
    chocolate

While the mince is cooking, heat a dash of oil in a large, deep, non-stick sauté pan over a medium heat and fry the onions and garlic for 8–10 minutes until softened. Stir in the ground spices and cook for 2–3 minutes to release their flavour.

Stir in the cooked mince and salami or chorizo. Cook for 2–3 minutes then pour in the reserved stock from the braised haunch. Add the kidney beans, give it a stir and bring to the boil. Lower the heat to a simmer and reduce the sauce until it's thick and stew-like, about 20 minutes.

Stir in the venison haunch and heat through for 5 minutes. Pour in the red wine, bring to the boil and add the lime zest. Lower the heat, season to taste and warm for a few minutes. Remove from the heat and stir in the chocolate.

Serve the venison chilli on warmed plates, with a dollop of crème fraîche and a little more chocolate grated over the top.

GREEN CHILLI CON CARNE

I've always been drawn to the raw flavour and heat you get from green chillies and green peppers and they're really great in this dish – mixing them with loads of fresh mint and lime makes for a lively and tasty combination. Unlike a regular chilli con carne, this one is dry in style and it's quite quick to make. SERVES 6–8

1kg minced pork
1 tbsp cumin seeds
1 tsp dried thyme
2 onions, diced
4 garlic cloves, finely grated
2 green peppers, cored,
    deseeded and diced
8 green chillies, chopped
    (seeds and all)
6 ripe tomatoes
150ml water
½ bunch of spring onions,
    trimmed and chopped
2 tsp salt, or to taste
1 tsp cracked black pepper
A bunch of mint, stalks
    removed, leaves shredded
Finely grated zest and juice
    of 2 unwaxed limes

To serve
Wholemilk yoghurt
Tortillas

Heat a large, non-stick frying pan over a medium-high heat. When it's hot, add the minced pork, cumin seeds and thyme and dry-fry for 10–15 minutes, breaking up the meat and stirring frequently, until it's dry, browned and crispy.

Using a slotted spoon, transfer the browned spicy meat to a bowl. Drain off any excess fat, keeping a little in the pan to cook the vegetables.

Return the pan to a medium-low heat. Add the onions and garlic and cook for about 10 minutes, stirring from time to time, until softened. Stir in the green peppers and chillies and cook for a further few minutes, then return the browned meat to the pan. Give everything a good stir and cook for another 5 minutes.

Meanwhile, deseed and roughly chop the tomatoes.

Pour the water into the pan, add the tomatoes and bring to the boil. Turn the heat to its lowest setting and let the chilli bubble away, uncovered, for around 15–25 minutes, until a lot of the liquid has evaporated. You want the mixture to be juicy but not too liquid and saucy.

Stir in the spring onions, salt and pepper. Finally, stir through the mint, and the lime zest and juice and allow to bubble for a couple of minutes longer. Take off the heat and leave to stand for 10 minutes to let the flavours develop before serving.

Spoon the chilli into warmed bowls and serve with plenty of yoghurt and tortillas, with a crisp green salad on the side if you like.

PULLED PORK SHOULDER

Over the past couple of years, this has become a very fashionable way to cook and serve pork and it's not hard to see why – it's easy and it's delicious! Seek out the best quality meat you can find and make sure it's on the bone – this helps to keep the meat moist and prevents too much shrinkage during the slow cooking process. In my version, I whack up the flavour by covering the pork in a lush rub at the beginning and adding a rich gravy at the end. SERVES 6–8

1 pork shoulder, skin
    removed, bone in,
    about 3kg

For the rub
1 tbsp black peppercorns
1 tbsp fennel seeds
1 tbsp coriander seeds
½ tbsp cumin seeds
1 tbsp smoked paprika
2 tsp garlic powder
1 tsp paprika
1 tsp cayenne pepper
1 tbsp dried oregano
1 tbsp dried sage
1 tbsp dried thyme
150g soft light brown sugar
1 tbsp salt

For the gravy
500g minced pork
2 onions, diced
6 garlic cloves, finely grated
100ml red wine vinegar
50g demerara sugar
200ml apple juice
2 tbsp black treacle
1 litre beef stock
75g Dijon mustard
2 tbsp Worcestershire sauce
2 tsp Tabasco sauce
Salt and freshly ground
    black pepper

First make the rub. Heat a small frying pan over a low heat and add the peppercorns and fennel, coriander and cumin seeds. Heat gently for a few minutes, shaking the pan to toast evenly, until the seeds are lightly golden and fragrant. Remove from the pan and let cool slightly, then grind to a fine powder using an electric spice grinder or pestle and mortar. Tip into a large bowl and stir in the remaining spices, herbs, sugar and salt.

Use your hands to massage the rub all over the pork shoulder, making sure it's completely coated. Wrap it in cling film and leave to stand for 1 hour.

Preheat the oven to 150°C/Fan 130°C/Gas 2.

Remove the cling film from the pork and place the shoulder on a wire rack set inside a large roasting tin. Roast for 4–5 hours, until the meat can be completed pulled away from the bone easily. It will be very soft and tender, but it will look dark and burnt – don't worry, it won't taste burnt I promise! Leave the pork to rest, loosely covered in foil, for around an hour.

In the meantime, make the gravy. Heat a large, non-stick frying pan or deep sauté pan over a medium-high heat. When hot, add the minced pork and dry-fry, stirring frequently, for around 10–15 minutes, until the meat is dry, brown and very crispy. Using a slotted spoon, transfer the mince from the pan to a bowl.

Return the pan to a medium heat. Add the onions and garlic and cook for about 10 minutes until softened, stirring from time to time. Add the wine vinegar and sugar, bring to the boil and let bubble to reduce to a glaze.

To serve (optional)
Buns

Once thickened, pour in the apple juice and treacle and let bubble until the sauce has once again reduced to a glaze and is lovely and syrupy.

Return the crispy mince to the pan, pour on the beef stock and bring back to the boil. Lower the heat and let bubble to reduce by half. Stir in the mustard, Worcestershire sauce, Tabasco and some salt and pepper. Give it a good stir and take off the heat.

Transfer the pork to a board and flake or 'pull' from the bone by prising the meat apart using a couple of forks. Place the shredded pork in a large bowl and gradually stir in the gravy a little at a time until it's coated nicely. You may not need to use it all (save any remaining gravy for another time). Taste and adjust the seasoning with salt and pepper if necessary.

Serve the pulled pork in buns for the ultimate sandwich, or with a crisp salad if you prefer.

PORK & FETA BURGER WITH CUCUMBER & OLIVE SALSA

I love pork and I love burgers! Pork belly is a perfect cut for mince as it has a great meat-to-fat ratio and it takes on other flavours beautifully. The salsa has a summery, vibrant flavour but these burgers are good simply with cheese and ketchup. MAKES 6

800g minced belly pork
2 garlic cloves, finely grated
3 green chillies, finely chopped (seeds and all)
½ tsp cracked black pepper
20 mint leaves, finely chopped
40g dried breadcrumbs
2 shallots, finely diced
70g green olives, pitted and chopped
½ tsp salt
150g feta cheese, crumbled
Olive oil, for frying

For the salsa
1 cucumber
4 spring onions, trimmed
½ bunch of dill, stalks removed, leaves finely chopped
3 tbsp olive oil
2 tbsp puréed green olives
1 green chilli, deseeded and finely chopped
Grated zest and juice of 1 small unwaxed lemon

To serve
Burger or brioche buns
Slices of cheese (optional)
Tomato ketchup (page 176) (optional)

To make the burgers, put all of the ingredients, except the oil, in a large bowl and mix thoroughly until well combined. Work together with your hands until the mixture forms a firm ball. Divide into 6 equal portions, shape into patties and place on a tray. Chill in the fridge for at least 30 minutes, or overnight if it's more convenient, to allow time for the flavours to develop.

Prepare the salsa about 20 minutes before you intend to serve the burgers. Peel the cucumber, halve lengthways and scoop out the seeds. Finely dice the cucumber flesh and place in a bowl. Thinly slice the spring onions and add to the cucumber along with all the other the ingredients. Toss to combine and set aside to allow the flavours to mingle.

When you're ready to cook the burgers, brush them with olive oil. Heat up your grill, barbecue or frying pan. You don't want to cook them on too fierce a heat, so turn the grill or pan down to medium, or cook the burgers towards the cooler edges of the barbecue.

Gently colour the burgers for 4–5 minutes on one side then flip them over and cook for a further 2 minutes or until cooked right through. Remove the burgers from the heat and leave to rest on a warmed plate for a couple of minutes.

Serve the burgers with the salsa sandwiched in buns, with cheese and/or tomato ketchup if you like.

ONE-POT HAM, SAUSAGE & PRAWN RICE

The trick to making this simple, fresh and colourful dish exceptional is layering the flavours one over another. Cooking and colouring the vegetables one batch at a time may seem like a bit of a pain, but the end result is well worth the graft. It's a real one-pot wonder! SERVES 4–6

½ cinnamon stick
½ tsp black peppercorns
2 cloves
2 bay leaves
Vegetable oil, for cooking
2 onions, diced
4 celery sticks (tough strings removed with a vegetable peeler), thinly sliced
1 green pepper, cored, deseeded and diced
1 fennel bulb, tough core removed, diced
200g cooked, smoked ham, cut into 2cm dice
200g garlic sausage, cut into 2cm dice
6 plum tomatoes, diced
4 garlic cloves, finely grated
2 tsp salt
2 tsp cayenne pepper
½ bunch of thyme, tied with kitchen string
175g basmati rice, rinsed
350ml chicken stock
250g peeled large raw prawns (tail shell intact), deveined
2 tbsp chopped parsley leaves
Salt and freshly ground black pepper

Wrap the cinnamon, peppercorns, cloves and bay leaves in a small piece of muslin and tie into a bundle with kitchen string.

Heat a splash of oil in a large, heavy-based flameproof casserole over a high heat. Add the onions and fry, stirring frequently, for 5–7 minutes until nicely browned. Remove and set aside.

Fry the celery, green pepper and fennel in the pan in separate batches, making sure they take on plenty of colour. You may need to add a dash more oil in between batches. Ensuring all the vegetables are beautifully caramelised helps to enrich the flavour of the finished dish, so don't skimp at this stage.

Once you've sautéed all of the vegetables and set them aside, add the ham to the pan and fry quickly to brown, then remove from the pan. Add the garlic sausage to the pan and sear on all sides until nicely browned too.

Return all of the sautéed vegetables and the ham to the pan. Give it a good stir then add the tomatoes, garlic, salt, cayenne, bunch of thyme and spice bag. Now add the rice and give everything a good stir to coat the rice in all the lovely flavours.

Pour in the stock and bring to the boil over a high heat. Lower the heat, cover and simmer very gently for 20–25 minutes until the rice has absorbed the liquid and is cooked through.

Add the prawns, give it a stir and cook for 4–5 minutes, just until the prawns have turned bright pink and are cooked through. Remove the spice bag and bunch of thyme. Scatter in the chopped parsley and taste for seasoning, adding more salt and pepper if needed. Serve immediately, in warmed bowls.

SIDES

'll be honest. I get quite excited about sides. Served alongside a special dish, they can make it spectacular if you get the combination of textures and flavours just right. Or they can transform a simple grilled steak or piece of fish into a great meal. And if you're strapped for time, several of them – such as the mac and cheese and stuffed green peppers – can be a meal in their own right.

Some of the recipes here are pretty simple – check out the crisp flatbreads and whole roast garlic. Once you have these in your repertoire, like me, you'll use them all the time. Others, like the dirty rice, have a longer list of ingredients and take a bit more effort, but I hope that these will become part of your everyday cooking too. Of course, you can change the seasonings and ingredients to suit your tastes and what you have in your kitchen cupboards. I'll be only too pleased if you do so and make these recipes your own.

I've also taken this opportunity to share with you my love of all things pickled. If you have a spare couple of hours, knock up a jar or two of soy-brined mushrooms, pickled carrots or pickled celery stalks. Serve them with some bread and cheese for a lovely simple lunch, or let them add their colour, flavour and texture to other more elaborate dishes. You can even scoop a bit of the pickling juice out of the jar and add it to marinades or dressings, or use it just as you would a squeeze of lemon to finish a dish, so nothing is wasted.

Side dishes are your chance to add a degree of complexity and contrast to the main event. If the key dish is roast or grilled meat, serve an unusual side that lends some crunch, such as rice and apple röstis; if it's spicy, calm it down a bit with cosy tomato and brown rice – you get the idea. Play around, mix and match, until you get the combination that is right for you.

CRISP FLATBREADS

These flatbreads are quick and simple to make. They're a great base for so many things – put a simple salad on top, spoon on some pulled pork shoulder (page 120), or smother with green chilli con carne (page 118). I'm sure you'll find loads of uses for them. MAKES 6–8

250g plain flour, plus extra
    for dusting
1 heaped tsp baking powder
½ tsp salt
150ml whole milk
Vegetable oil, for frying
Flaky sea salt

Mix the flour, baking powder and salt together in a large bowl. Make a well in the centre, add the milk and use your hands to slowly bring the mixture together to form a dough.

Knead the dough in the bowl for a couple of minutes to work into a ball. Cover with cling film and leave to rest at room temperature for 15–30 minutes.

Form the rested dough into egg-sized balls. On a lightly floured surface, roll each one out thinly until about the size of a side plate. Pierce a couple of times with a fork.

Heat around a 2cm depth of oil in a large, deep sauté pan or heavy-based saucepan over a medium heat to 180°C. Use a frying thermometer to check the temperature, if you have one; otherwise drop a cube of dry white bread into the hot oil to test it – if the bread cube turns golden brown in just under a minute, the oil is ready.

Carefully fry the flatbreads, one at a time, for 2–3 minutes on each side until lightly golden and crisp, turning carefully with tongs. Remove and drain on kitchen paper. Keep warm in a low oven while you fry the remaining breads, making sure the oil comes back up to temperature between each one.

Scatter a little sea salt over the flatbreads just before serving.

SAUTÉED CHICKPEAS WITH CHEESE & BACON

One of the things I really like about this dish is that I usually have all the ingredients knocking around in the fridge or cupboards, so I can make a batch whenever I fancy. It's a great alternative to mash and, as it's rich and filling, a little goes a long way. It can even make a nice quick supper on its own with a leafy salad, or try serving it alongside a steak or sausages, or with the dry-rub beef ribs (page 100) or weekend roast chicken (page 76). SERVES 4

50g butter
200g smoked lardons or
    diced smoked bacon
1 onion, diced
2 garlic cloves, finely grated
400g tin chickpeas, drained
    (liquid reserved) and
    rinsed
75g crème fraîche
200g strong Cheddar cheese,
    grated
2 tbsp chopped chives
Salt and freshly ground
    black pepper

Melt the butter in a large, non-stick frying pan over a medium heat. Add the lardons or bacon pieces and sauté for around 5 minutes until the fat is rendered and they have taken on some colour.

Add the onion and garlic, reduce the heat and continue to cook for a further 10 minutes, stirring from time to time, until the onion has softened but hasn't taken on any colour.

Add the chickpeas to the pan, and allow to cook very gently for 8–10 minutes so that they take on the bacon and onion flavours. Towards the end of cooking, stir in a little of the reserved liquid from the chickpea tin, to loosen the mixture.

Using a fork or a potato masher, gently crush the chickpeas in the pan to form a coarse purée, leaving some whole. Season to taste with salt and pepper. Take off the heat and stir in the crème fraîche, cheese and half of the chives.

Spoon into a serving dish and scatter the remaining chives on top just before serving.

RICE & APPLE RÖSTIS

These are a tasty twist on a classic potato rösti. Nice and crisp on the outside and soft and full of flavour on the inside, they're great served simply with fried eggs, or as an accompaniment to almost any roast meat. Try them with tea-brined roast duck (page 90), weekend roast chicken (page 76) or spiced roast rump of lamb (page 92).
MAKES 8

100g cashew nuts
200g wild rice, cooked until very tender (this often takes longer than you think – up to an hour)
200g basmati rice, cooked
1 Granny Smith apple, peeled, cored and grated
3 tbsp chopped chervil or parsley
½ tsp ground nutmeg
Finely grated zest of 1 small unwaxed orange
60g plain flour
1 egg, lightly beaten
A splash of milk, if necessary
Vegetable oil, for frying
Salt and freshly ground black pepper

Preheat the oven to 180°C/Fan 160°C/Gas 4. Scatter the cashew nuts on a baking tray and place in the oven for 8–10 minutes until fragrant and lightly toasted. Tip onto on a board and allow to cool. Chop the cashews coarsely and set aside.

Place the wild and basmati rice in a large bowl and add the cashews, grated apple, herbs, nutmeg and orange zest. Season generously with salt and pepper and stir to combine.

Sift the flour over the mixture, then mix thoroughly again. You want to make sure the flour is well distributed throughout the mixture. Add the beaten egg and mix well to bind, adding a splash of milk to loosen the mixture slightly, if necessary.

Divide the mixture into 8 portions and roll into balls. Shape these into little cakes, patting and compressing the mixture with your hands so that the cakes hold their shape. Place on a plate, cover with cling film and chill in the fridge for 1 hour to firm up.

You will probably need to cook the röstis in batches to avoid overcrowding the pan. Heat a glug of oil in a large, non-stick frying pan over a medium-high heat. When hot, add the röstis and cook for 2–3 minutes on each side, until nicely golden brown and crisp on both sides. Drain on kitchen paper and keep them warm while you cook the rest.

Serve the rice and apple röstis on warmed plates as soon as they are all cooked.

DIRTY RICE

Talk about a big mix of flavours! I use minced pork, smoked bacon, chicken livers and lots of peppers, garlic and spices here, but feel free to change the ingredients as you like. It's a great accompaniment to barbecued food. Try it with blackened Cajun redfish (page 67) or dry-rub beef ribs (page 100). SERVES 4–6

250g chicken livers, cleaned and trimmed
Vegetable oil, for frying
200g smoked lardons or diced smoked bacon
250g minced pork
2 celery sticks (tough strings removed with a vegetable peeler), diced
1 onion, diced
1 green pepper, cored, deseeded and diced
1 red pepper, cored, deseeded and diced
4 garlic cloves, finely grated
2 green chillies, chopped (seeds and all)
2 bay leaves
1 tsp dried thyme
1 tsp cracked black pepper
1 cinnamon stick
200g basmati rice
350ml chicken stock
A small bunch of parsley, tough stems removed, leaves chopped
A few spring onions, trimmed and finely sliced
Salt

First cook the chicken livers. Heat a splash of oil in a large, non-stick saucepan over a high heat. Once it is hot, add the chicken livers and fry quickly, for about 1–2 minutes on each side until they are nicely golden; be careful not to overcook them. Transfer the livers to a plate to cool.

Return the pan to a medium-high heat and add the bacon. Cook for a few minutes, stirring frequently, until it is crisp and golden brown all over. Using a slotted spoon, remove the bacon from the pan and set aside on a plate (not the one holding the chicken livers). Make sure you leave all of the cooking fat and juices in the pan.

Tip the minced pork into the pan and fry over a medium-high heat for about 10 minutes, stirring from time to time, until it's very crispy. Using a slotted spoon, transfer the mince from the pan to the plate with the bacon, again leaving as much fat in the pan as possible. Reduce the heat to medium-low.

Add the celery, onion, peppers, garlic and chillies to the pan and sauté gently for 8–10 minutes, until softened. Stir in the bay leaves, thyme, black pepper and cinnamon stick. Heat for a further minute, then add the rice and stir to coat.

Return the pork and bacon to the pan. Pour on the chicken stock, whack up the heat and bring to the boil. Lower the heat to a simmer and cook gently for about 15 minutes, until the stock has been absorbed and the rice is cooked through.

Meanwhile, coarsely chop the chicken livers. When the rice is ready, gently stir through the chopped livers, parsley and spring onions. Taste and season with a little salt if necessary. Pile the rice into a warmed serving dish and serve at once.

TOMATO & BROWN RICE

This is a very versatile rice dish, which goes with so many things. Enjoy it hot with grilled fish, roasts or slow-cooked meats, or cold, dressed in a little good olive oil and vinegar or lemon juice. Hot or cold, you can add other vegetables as you wish – peas, asparagus, roasted peppers, spring onions are all good, but I'm sure you'll come up with your own favourites too. SERVES 4–6

Vegetable oil, for cooking
250g smoked streaky bacon,
    cut into lardons
1 large onion, diced
2 garlic cloves, finely grated
½ tsp dried sage
½ tsp dried thyme
1 chicken stock cube
250g long-grain brown rice
1 tsp tomato purée
½ tsp cayenne pepper
150ml water
400g tin chopped tomatoes
75g sun-dried tomatoes,
    roughly chopped
1 ball of mozzarella, about
    125g, diced
Salt and freshly ground
    black pepper

Heat a drizzle of oil in a large, deep non-stick sauté pan or saucepan over a medium-high heat. Add the bacon and sauté for about 4-5 minutes, until golden brown and crisp.

Lower the heat and add the onion and garlic. Cook gently, stirring from time to time, until the onion has softened but not taken on any colour; this will take around 10-15 minutes.

Add the sage and thyme, then crumble in the stock cube. Stir in the brown rice, making sure it's well coated in all of the seasonings. Add the tomato purée and cayenne pepper and continue to cook for another minute or two. Pour in the water and tip in the tinned tomatoes.

Increase the heat and bring to the boil, then turn down to a simmer and cook, uncovered, for about 15-20 minutes until all of the liquid has been absorbed and the rice is tender. You may need to cook it for a further few minutes depending on the rice – be guided by the packet instructions. You want the rice still to have a slight bite to it, and a lovely, nutty flavour.

Remove from the heat, then add the sun-dried tomatoes and mozzarella and fork through, so the cheese starts to melt into the rice. Season with salt and pepper to taste and serve.

CHEESY POLENTA DOUGHNUTS

These tasty little savoury doughnuts make a great starter or snack, or you can serve them as an accompaniment to fried fish dishes, such as seared sea bass with roasted pepper salsa (page 62) or sunflower seed crusted sea trout (page 64). I use a mixture of beer and buttermilk to bind the batter, but you could just use one or the other if you like. SERVES 6–8

300g fine polenta
100g self-raising flour
100g Parmesan cheese,
    finely grated
A bunch of chives, finely
    chopped
1 tsp salt
½ tsp baking powder
150ml buttermilk
150ml beer (I like to use
    a wheat beer)
1 egg, lightly beaten
Vegetable oil, for frying
Flaky sea salt, to finish

Put the polenta, flour, grated Parmesan, chives, salt and baking powder into a large bowl. Mix to combine, then make a well in the centre.

In a separate bowl, whisk together the buttermilk, beer and egg. Gradually whisk this liquid mix into the dry ingredients to form a batter. Leave to rest at room temperature for about 10–15 minutes.

Heat about a 15cm depth of oil in a deep-fat fryer to 180°C. Or use a large, deep pan, making sure it is no more than a third full as the oil will bubble up ferociously when you add the batter. Use a frying thermometer to check the temperature, if you have one; otherwise drop a cube of dry white bread into the hot oil to test it – if it turns golden brown in just under a minute, the oil is up to temperature. Keep a close eye on it and never leave the pan unattended, even for a minute.

You will need to fry the doughnuts in batches. Don't overcrowd the pan, and allow the oil to come back up to temperature between batches. Shape the batter into quenelles (neat ovals) by passing each large spoonful between two tablespoons and then carefully lower into the hot oil. Cook for 3–4 minutes, turning as necessary, until the doughnuts are golden brown and deliciously crisp.

Remove the doughnuts from the oil using a slotted spoon and drain on a plate or tray lined with kitchen paper. Scatter with a little flaky sea salt and serve immediately.

MAC & CHEESE

Is there anything more satisfying than macaroni cheese? In my version, I use four different cheeses – Cheddar for its strength of flavour, Gruyère for its elasticity, mozzarella for its texture and Parmesan for crunch! Serve it with everything from roasts to burgers, or on its own with a crisp salad. SERVES 4–6

500g dried macaroni

For the cheese sauce
500ml whole milk
A bunch of rosemary, tied
    with kitchen string
2 bay leaves
35g butter, plus extra for
    greasing the dish
35g plain flour
1 tbsp English mustard
    powder
1 tsp ground mace
150g strong Cheddar cheese,
    grated
100g Gruyère cheese, grated
2 garlic cloves, finely grated
1 ball of buffalo mozzarella,
    about 125g, diced
Salt and freshly ground
    black pepper

For the topping
100g fresh breadcrumbs
100g Parmesan cheese,
    freshly grated
1 tsp smoked paprika

Preheat the oven to 180°C/Fan 160°C/Gas 4. Lightly butter an ovenproof dish, about 30 x 25cm and 7cm deep.

Bring a large saucepan of salted water to the boil and cook the macaroni for 8–10 minutes until *al dente* (cooked but still with a bite), especially as it will be going into the oven. Drain in a colander, run briefly under cold water and set aside.

To make the cheese sauce, put the milk, rosemary and bay leaves into a medium saucepan and slowly bring to a simmer. As soon as it begins to bubble, remove from the heat and set aside to infuse for 15 minutes. Pour the infused milk through a sieve over a jug to strain out the herbs.

Melt the butter in a separate, large saucepan over a medium-low heat. Once it stops foaming, reduce the heat slightly and add the flour, mustard powder and mace. Cook for 3–4 minutes, stirring continuously, to cook out the flour.

Slowly pour in the infused milk, a little at a time, whisking constantly to keep the sauce smooth. Simmer gently for a few minutes, stirring all the time, until thickened. Lower the heat and add the Cheddar and Gruyère, and the garlic. Stir until the cheese has melted, then season well with salt and pepper.

Remove from the heat and add the cooked macaroni to the cheese sauce, stirring to coat it evenly. Fold in the mozzarella then pour into the prepared ovenproof dish.

For the topping, mix the breadcrumbs, Parmesan and smoked paprika together in a bowl. Scatter over the macaroni cheese and place the dish on a baking tray.

Bake for 20–25 minutes, until the topping is golden brown, crisp and bubbling. Let stand for 5 minutes before serving.

STUFFED GREEN PEPPERS

I like to serve these as an accompaniment to a barbecue, or as part of any sort of help-yourself feast. In this recipe, I stuff the peppers with minced beef but you can replace that with any other minced meat, or with cooked rice or diced mushrooms for a vegetarian dish. SERVES 6

6 large green peppers
750g minced beef
150g butter
2 large onions, diced
2 garlic cloves, finely grated
300g strong Cheddar cheese, grated
150g fresh breadcrumbs
3 eggs, lightly beaten
4 tbsp Bovril
2 tbsp chopped oregano leaves
Extra virgin olive oil, to drizzle
Salt and freshly ground black pepper

To prepare the peppers, stand one upright on a board and cut about 1cm off the top, then use a spoon to scoop out the seeds and membrane. Repeat with the rest of the peppers. Give the inside of the peppers a quick rinse under the cold tap to dislodge any stray seeds.

Heat a large, non-stick frying pan over a medium-high heat, then add the minced beef, breaking it up with a wooden spoon. Dry-fry for about 25 minutes, stirring frequently, until it is well browned and crispy. Tip the mince into a colander to drain off the excess fat, then transfer to a large bowl and set aside. Wipe the pan clean with kitchen paper.

Preheat the oven to 180°C/Fan 160°C/Gas 4.

Return the pan to a medium-low heat and add the butter. Once it's stopped foaming, add the onions and garlic and cook gently for about 12–15 minutes, stirring from time to time, until the onions are softened and translucent. Remove from the heat and add to the bowl with the beef.

Once the onions have cooled slightly, stir in three-quarters of the cheese, three-quarters of the breadcrumbs, the eggs, Bovril and oregano. Mix well to combine. Taste, then season with salt and pepper.

Spoon the stuffing mixture into the peppers, dividing it evenly. Stand them in an ovenproof dish – one that will hold them snugly, so they can stand upright. Sprinkle with the remaining cheese and breadcrumbs and drizzle over a little olive oil.

Cover the dish tightly with foil. Bake the stuffed peppers for 40 minutes, then remove the foil and return to the oven for a further 15–20 minutes until the tops are browned and crunchy. Let stand for a few minutes before serving.

SOY-BRINED MUSHROOMS

These mushrooms are brilliant to have on standby in the fridge. The dark soy really enhances and deepens their naturally earthy, savoury flavour. They add body and substance to salads, perk up casseroles and are delicious chopped up and stirred into risottos. They're also lovely eaten just on their own, as a snack. I like to add them to a deep-pan meat feast pizza (page 108) and one-pot ham, sausage and prawn rice (page 124), or serve them as an accompaniment to my beef and beer loaf (page 102).
MAKES ABOUT 1.5kg

1kg portobellini or chestnut
    mushrooms
Vegetable oil, for cooking
4 garlic cloves, peeled and
    bashed slightly
3 banana shallots, thinly
    sliced

For the soy brine
1 litre water
250ml dark soy sauce
200ml white wine vinegar
100g caster sugar
100g dried ceps or porcini
3 star anise
3 bay leaves
1 stick of liquorice root
    (available from health
    food shops or online)
A small bunch of thyme, tied
    with kitchen string

To prepare the mushrooms, gently twist the stems of any larger mushrooms to release them and discard; leave smaller ones intact. Halve the mushrooms or thickly slice them.

Heat a large, non-stick frying pan over a high heat and add a dash of oil. Once hot, sear the fresh mushrooms in batches for a minute or two – you want them to keep their shape and texture so don't cook them for too long or heat them all the way through. Remove the mushrooms from the pan using a slotted spoon and set aside while you prepare the soy brine.

Put the water, soy sauce, wine vinegar and sugar into a large saucepan and heat, stirring to dissolve the sugar, then bring to the boil. Drop in the dried mushrooms, star anise, bay leaves, liquorice root and thyme. Reduce the heat and simmer gently for 4–5 minutes.

Take off the heat and stir in the bashed garlic cloves, sliced shallots and fried mushrooms. Leave to cool.

Once cooled, transfer to sterilised jars and store in the fridge until ready to use. The mushrooms will keep in the fridge for 2 weeks.

PICKLED CARROTS WITH ORANGE & CARDAMOM

These pickled carrots are awesome! Crisp and crunchy with a fragrant citrus kick from the orange zest, I often eat them on their own, but they're a really good addition to other dishes too. I like them as an accompaniment to buffalo chicken wings (page 28), pulled pork shoulder (page 120), and blackened Cajun redfish (page 67). Essentially, they add an extra dimension to spicy or rich dishes. MAKES ABOUT 1kg

6 large carrots
3 banana shallots
30g flaky sea salt
30g caster sugar

For the pickling liquor
250ml water
250ml cider vinegar
150g demerara sugar
2 lime leaves
Finely pared zest of
    1 unwaxed orange, peeled
    in strips with a vegetable
    peeler
1 tsp cardamom pods, lightly
    crushed
1 tsp black peppercorns
2 star anise

Peel the carrots and slice lengthways on an angle, into 3mm thick slices. Peel and slice the banana shallots in the same way and tip both into a large bowl. Sprinkle with the salt and sugar and mix together well. Leave to stand for about 10 minutes.

Tip the carrots and shallots into a colander and rinse them briefly under cold running water to remove the salt. Shake well to dry and then transfer to a clean, large bowl.

For the pickling liquor, pour the water and cider vinegar into a medium saucepan. Add the demerara sugar, lime leaves, orange zest, cardamom pods, peppercorns and star anise. Place over a medium-high heat, stirring to dissolve the sugar, and bring to the boil.

Immediately pour the hot pickling liquor over the carrots and shallots. Cover with cling film and set aside to cool.

Once cooled, transfer the carrots, shallots and pickling liquor to cold, sterilised jars and refrigerate for at least 3 days before eating so all the lovely flavours develop and intensify. The pickle will keep in the fridge for 2 weeks.

PICKLED CELERY STALKS

I'm a massive fan of celery. There's so much more to it than something you chop up and use as the base for a soup or stew. Sometimes I like to make it the main event, to take advantage of its lovely floral, botanical flavours. These pickled celery stalks are great simply served with cheese or as a big part of a salad, but they also act as a foil to rich stews or slow-cooked barbecue meats. Try them with dry-rub beef ribs (page 100). You'll need to prepare this dish 2 to 3 days before you want to eat it, but it'll keep for a couple of weeks in the fridge. MAKES ABOUT 750g

1 head of celery

For the pickling liquor
350ml water
150ml white wine vinegar
175g caster sugar
20g salt
2 garlic cloves, skin on and
    lightly crushed
2 bay leaves
1 tsp coriander seeds
1 tsp fennel seeds
1 tsp black peppercorns
2 star anise
½ tsp cardamom pods,
    lightly crushed
Finely pared zest of 1 small
    unwaxed lemon, peeled
    in strips with a vegetable
    peeler

To prepare the celery, cut off the root and separate the sticks. Rinse them under the cold tap, then run a vegetable peeler over each one to get rid of the tough outer strings. Cut the sticks into lengths that will fit upright in the jar(s) you're going to pickle them in. Place them in a large bowl.

To prepare the pickling liquor, put the water into a medium saucepan and add all of the remaining ingredients, except the lemon zest. Heat, stirring to dissolve the sugar and salt. Bring to a rolling boil, lower the heat and simmer for 3–4 minutes. Remove from the heat and pour the pickling liquor through a fine sieve onto the celery.

Add the strips of lemon zest to the bowl, along with a few of the aromatics from the pickling liquor – a bay leaf, a star anise, a few peppercorns, a couple of cardamom pods and a pinch of fennel seeds should do it. Cover the bowl with cling film and set aside to cool.

Once cool, transfer the celery pickle to cold, sterilised jars and refrigerate for at least 2 days before serving. It will keep in the fridge for 2 weeks.

WHOLE ROAST GARLIC

This is such a simple way of cooking garlic – if you haven't tried it before, the rich, mellow and slightly sweet flavour of roasted garlic is near addictive. You can serve it as a simple side dish with steaks or roasts, or scoop out the flesh from the skins and beat it into butter or cream cheese, or fold through pasta or bake in a bread dough. Roasted garlic is so versatile, I'm sure you'll find lots of uses for it. SERVES 6

6 whole garlic bulbs
½ bunch of flat-leaf parsley,
    stalks only
½ tsp ground mace
2 tsp flaky sea salt
A bunch of thyme
200ml olive oil

Preheat the oven to 180°C/Fan 160°C/Gas 4.

Cut the garlic bulbs in half horizontally, through their equator. Line a small roasting tray with foil and scatter the parsley stalks over the base. Sit the garlic halves on top, cut sides facing upwards, and sprinkle with the mace and salt. Scatter over the thyme sprigs and drizzle with the olive oil.

Place another sheet of foil on top and scrunch the edges together all around to make a well-sealed parcel. Bake for 40 minutes, until the garlic is softened. Remove from the oven and leave to cool slightly.

Serve the garlic halves hot, as they are, or scoop out the flesh and use in savoury butters, sauces and breads.

You can also push the soft garlic cloves out of the skin into a cold, sterilised jar and pour over some olive oil to cover, then seal and store in the fridge for up to a week.

SAUCES & RELISHES

'll jump at any chance to add more flavour. I just can't help myself. These recipes represent some of my best, tried-and-tested, go-to ways to turbo-charge other dishes and give them a real flavour boost. If you have an hour or so to spare and you fancy messing about in the kitchen, have a go at putting a few of these sauces and relishes together. It's like storing up flavour, if not for a rainy day exactly, then at least for a hungry one.

Lots of them are great with other recipes in this book. Stir a bit of barbecue sauce into a venison chilli, or brush some tomato ketchup over the top of the beef and beer loaf before you put it in the oven to get a beautiful caramelised crust. Or splash some mushroom ketchup into the milk gravy to go with pan-roasted chicken to give an extra layer of flavour. Spoon some guacamole or one or more of the fresh salsas alongside one of the slow-cooked meat dishes, such as the pulled pork shoulder, to balance out the rich, deep flavours of the meat. They will lift everything to a new level.

So yes, of course, I hope you pair some of these recipes with the other dishes in this book. But I'd really love it if you used them to perk up your regular, everyday dinners too, to give familiar dishes a bit of a makeover. Preparing a simple roast chicken or meat loaf? Try it with some bacon and treacle sauce. Spoon a bit of spicy apple sauce alongside a gammon steak or spread some green tomato relish under a round of cheese on toast to give it a bit of zip.

Any time you can put in now will be well rewarded later, as these sauces and relishes make it super-easy to throw together a really tasty lunch or dinner with the minimum of effort. Give them a go – you'll be glad you did.

BACON & TREACLE SAUCE

This is a rich and powerful gravy, with a deliciously smoky flavour from the lardons. It goes really well with roasted red meats and game, or with sausages or roasted root vegetables, and anything cooked over coals. I even like it with fish – try it with seared sea bass (page 62) or sunflower seed crusted sea trout (page 64). The sauce freezes well too, so it's worth scaling up the quantities so you have a batch on hand in the freezer to pep up a simple supper. MAKES ABOUT 600ml

200g smoked lardons or diced smoked bacon
2 banana shallots, finely diced
1 garlic clove, finely grated
175ml cider vinegar
2 tbsp black treacle
200ml beef stock
75ml olive oil
1 tbsp thyme leaves
2 tbsp chopped chives
Salt and freshly ground black pepper

Heat a deep sauté pan over a medium-high heat then add the lardons or bacon. Fry for 4–5 minutes, stirring frequently, until golden brown and crispy. Stir in the shallots and garlic, lower the heat and cook for 8–10 minutes until they have softened.

Pour the cider vinegar into the pan, turn up the heat and let the liquid bubble to reduce until thickened to a syrupy glaze. Stir in the black treacle and then pour in the beef stock.

Bring to the boil, reduce the heat and let the sauce simmer gently, uncovered, for about 10 minutes to reduce and thicken until it nicely coats the back of a wooden spoon. Whisk in the olive oil to emulsify and enrich the sauce. Stir in the thyme and chives and warm through for a minute.

Remove from the heat and season the sauce to taste with salt and pepper. Serve immediately, in a warmed jug or sauceboat. Alternatively, it can be kept in a sealed container in the fridge for 3 days, or frozen until needed.

SPICY APPLE SAUCE

Everyone should have a good apple sauce in their repertoire, and this is mine. It's a wonderful combination of mild spice, sweetness and acidity and is great spooned onto all sorts of roasted meats, especially pork, or even fish. Try it with pulled pork shoulder (page 120), pork and feta burgers (page 122), sunflower seed crusted sea trout (page 64) or Cajun blackened redfish (page 67). It is delicious hot or cold.
MAKES ABOUT 650g

Vegetable oil, for cooking
1 onion, finely diced
2 Bramley apples, about
    800g in total
½ tsp ground cinnamon
½ tsp ground mace
½ tsp ground ginger
½ tsp freshly ground
    black pepper
70g caster sugar
150ml water
Juice of 1 lemon

Heat a splash of oil in a medium saucepan over a medium heat. Add the onion and cook, stirring from time to time, for 8-10 minutes until softened. Meanwhile, peel, core and coarsely grate the apples.

Sprinkle the cinnamon, mace, ginger and pepper over the onion and cook gently for a further 2–3 minutes, to let the spice flavours blend.

Stir in the sugar, water and lemon juice, then increase the heat and bring to the boil. Once bubbling, add the grated apples, reduce the heat to a bare simmer and cook gently for around 10 minutes, stirring frequently until the apple is soft.

Remove from the heat and let cool for a few minutes, then transfer to a jug blender or food processor. Whiz until smooth then pass the sauce through a fine sieve into a serving bowl.

Serve immediately, or keep the sauce in a sealed container in the fridge until ready to use. It will keep for up to a week.

GREEN TOMATO RELISH

Under-ripe green tomatoes lack the sweetness that comes from a sun-ripened, warm, red tomato, but they do offer a fantastic 'raw' edge of bitterness that goes so well in a relish. This is a great accompaniment to cheeses and smoked meats, but try it with more complex dishes too, such as Cajun blackened redfish (page 67), pulled pork shoulder (page 120) or marinated lamb ribs with roasted onions (page 96).

MAKES ABOUT 2.2kg

500g green tomatoes, chopped
500g onions, finely diced
500g green cabbage, finely sliced
4 green peppers, cored, deseeded and diced
2 red peppers, cored, deseeded and diced
2 green chillies, chopped (seeds and all)
250g caster sugar
50g salt
400ml cider vinegar
150ml water
2 tbsp yellow mustard seeds
2 tbsp fennel seeds
½ tsp ground turmeric

In a large bowl, mix together the green tomatoes, onions, cabbage, peppers and chillies. Add the sugar and salt and stir to mix thoroughly. Cover the bowl with cling film and refrigerate overnight.

The next day, tip all of the vegetables into a colander and rinse under cold running water to remove the salt and sugar. Set aside.

Put the cider vinegar, water, mustard and fennel seeds and the turmeric into a large saucepan and bring to the boil. Add the vegetables, stir and take off the heat. Leave the vegetables to cool down in the liquor.

Once cooled, transfer the vegetables and liquor to cold, sterilised jars. Seal and store in the fridge until ready to serve. Sealed jars will keep nicely for up to 2 months; once opened consume within 2 weeks.

GUACAMOLE

Rich, creamy and spicy, this guacamole takes minutes to throw together but it's so satisfying and delicious to eat, either on its own with a few tortilla chips, or as an accompaniment to another dish. This is a more elaborate and punchy version of the guacamole in my spicy king prawns and salsa recipe (page 42), but either would go beautifully with Cajun blackened redfish (page 67) or green chilli con carne (page 118). Avocados discolour quite quickly, so enjoy your guacamole as soon as possible after you've made it. SERVES 6

4 plum tomatoes
2 ripe avocados
3 tbsp lemon juice
Finely grated zest of
    1 unwaxed lime
1 small red onion, finely
    diced
2 red chillies, chopped
    (seeds and all)
2 tbsp Worcestershire sauce
2 tbsp chopped coriander
    leaves
Salt and freshly ground
    black pepper

To prepare the tomatoes, have a bowl of iced water ready and bring a saucepan of water to the boil. Blanch the tomatoes in the boiling water for 10–15 seconds then immediately plunge into the iced water to stop them cooking. Skin the tomatoes and chop the flesh; set aside.

Halve the avocados and use a spoon to scoop out the flesh into a bowl. Immediately spoon on the lemon juice to prevent the avocado from browning and add the lime zest. Mash together lightly with a fork, keeping a little texture – you want it to be fairly chunky.

Add the tomatoes, onion, chillies, Worcestershire sauce and coriander and toss gently to combine. Season to taste with salt and pepper. Transfer to a dish and serve immediately.

SALSAS

I love salsas. I've started to view them as a very important part of my cooking as they can bring a great balance of acidity, spice, sweetness and texture to all kinds of dishes. I'm sharing five of my favourite recipes here. I hope you'll give them a go, and that they inspire you to create favourite combinations of your own.

POMEGRANATE, CHILLI & RED PEPPER SALSA

The crunch and sweet-sour flavour of pomegranates work brilliantly with the heat from chillies and the lively freshness of herbs. This salsa is very good with simply grilled or fried fish, or my Cajun blackened redfish (page 67). I really like it with pulled pork shoulder (page 120) too. SERVES 6–8

1 pomegranate
1 red onion, finely chopped
1 red pepper, cored, deseeded
　　and finely diced
2 red chillies, finely chopped
　　(seeds and all)
A bunch of coriander,
　　roughly chopped (stalks
　　and all)
½ bunch of mint, stalks
　　removed, leaves roughly
　　chopped
½ bunch of flat-leaf parsley,
　　stalks removed, leaves
　　roughly chopped
Grated zest and juice of
　　1 unwaxed lime
Olive oil, to bind
Salt and freshly ground
　　black pepper

To prepare the pomegranate, cut it in half across the middle and, using a fork or spoon, bash the outside skin on each half over a bowl, until all of the seeds have been released into the bowl. Pick out and discard any bitter membrane that accidentally falls into the bowl.

Stir in all the remaining ingredients, adding just enough olive oil to coat everything and loosen the salsa. Season with salt and pepper to taste.

Cover with cling film and refrigerate until needed. This salsa is best eaten within a few hours of making.

Illustrated overleaf

CUCUMBER, CUMIN & MINT SALSA

This cooling and refreshing salsa is great with all kinds of fish and seafood dishes, including crab cakes (page 48) and sunflower seed crusted sea trout (page 64). I like it with spiced roast rump of lamb (page 92) too. SERVES 6

1 cucumber
4 celery sticks
1 tbsp flaky sea salt
1½ tbsp cumin seeds
A bunch of mint, stalks
    removed, leaves chopped
½ bunch of coriander,
    chopped (stalks and all)
Grated zest and juice of
    1 unwaxed lime
Grated zest and juice of
    1 unwaxed lemon
1 tbsp soft dark brown sugar
1 onion, finely diced
1 garlic clove, finely grated
Olive oil, to bind
Salt and freshly ground
    black pepper

Halve the cucumber lengthways, scoop out the seeds and finely dice the flesh. Peel away the tough strings from the celery with a vegetable peeler then finely dice. Combine the cucumber and celery in a bowl and scatter over the flaky salt. Toss well to coat and leave to stand for 20 minutes.

Meanwhile, lightly toast the cumin seeds in a small, dry frying pan over a medium-high heat for a few minutes, shaking the pan from time to time, until fragrant. Leave to cool.

Using a pestle and mortar, bash the mint, coriander, lime and lemon zests and the brown sugar together until crushed to a paste, releasing the flavours.

Tip the cucumber and celery into a colander and rinse off the salt under cold running water. Pat dry with kitchen paper then place in a large, clean bowl.

Stir in the onion, garlic, toasted cumin, lime juice and crushed herb mixture. Mix in enough olive oil to coat everything and loosen the salsa. Season to taste with salt and pepper and add a dash of lemon juice if it needs that extra acidity.

Cover with cling film and chill until needed. This salsa is best eaten within a few hours of making.

Illustrated overleaf

Clockwise (from top left):
Tomato & chilli salsa; Mango & red onion salsa; Sweetcorn & black bean salsa; Cucumber, cumin & mint salsa; Pomegranate, chilli & red pepper salsa

MANGO & RED ONION SALSA

I love the perfumed sweetness that comes from mango, combined with the sharpness of the onion and the heat of the chillies. This salsa works brilliantly with all sorts of cooked meats, hot or cold. Try it with fish too – it's particularly good with Cajun blackened redfish (page 67) and seared sea bass (page 62). SERVES 6–8

2 ripe mangoes
2 red onions, finely diced
1 large red pepper, cored,
    deseeded and finely diced
3 jalapeno peppers, sliced
    (with seeds)
2 tbsp olive oil
Juice of 1 orange
Pinch of salt

To prepare the mangoes, peel and slice them around the stone as closely as possible to release the flesh, then dice it. Transfer to a large bowl and stir in the rest of the ingredients.

Cover with cling film and keep in the fridge until needed. This salsa is best eaten within a couple of hours of preparing.

Illustrated on preceding pages

TOMATO & CHILLI SALSA

This is one of my favourite salsas, great on its own with some tortilla chips or as an accompaniment to barbecued dishes, slow-cooked meats, or grilled or fried fish. SERVES 6

10 ripe plum tomatoes,
    roughly chopped
3 red chillies, chopped
    (seeds and all)
3 garlic cloves, finely grated
1 onion, diced
1 tbsp chopped oregano
    leaves
2 tbsp white wine vinegar
2 tbsp chopped sun-dried
    tomatoes
1 tbsp caster sugar
1 tsp salt
1 tsp freshly ground white
    (or black) pepper

Put all the ingredients into a food processor and pulse until well combined. Be careful not to overwork – you want the salsa to have some texture.

Transfer the salsa to a serving dish, cover with cling film and keep in the fridge until needed. It will keep for up to a day, but like all salsas it's best eaten soon after it's made.

Illustrated on preceding pages

SWEETCORN & BLACK BEAN SALSA

This salsa has a wonderful savoury flavour running through, but also the sweetness that I really think you need in a salsa from the sweetcorn. This is great with any kind of barbecued food. SERVES 6–8

3 corn-on-the-cobs, husks
and silky threads removed
400g tin black beans, drained
and rinsed
2 plum tomatoes, chopped
1 red onion, finely diced
1 red pepper, cored, deseeded
and finely diced
2 red chillies, finely chopped
(seeds and all)
Grated zest and juice of
2 unwaxed limes
½ bunch of coriander,
roughly chopped (stalks
and all)
100ml olive oil
Salt and freshly ground
black pepper

Bring a large saucepan of water to the boil, and add the corn-on-the-cobs. Boil for about 5–6 minutes, until the kernels are tender. Remove the cobs from the pan and set aside to cool.

Once cool enough to handle, run a sharp knife run down the length of each cob to release the kernels. Place them in a large bowl and stir in the rest of the ingredients. Season to taste with salt and pepper.

Cover with cling film and refrigerate until needed. For the best flavour, eat within a couple of hours.

Illustrated on preceding pages

BARBECUE SAUCE

This is a fantastic sauce to serve with burgers, sausages or any other barbecued meat, but it's also great with scrambled eggs or a full English breakfast. Try it with pork and feta burgers (page 122), beef and beer loaf (page 102) or pulled pork shoulder (page 120). MAKES ABOUT 450ml

For the spice mix
1 tsp yellow mustard seeds
1 tsp fennel seeds
1 tsp cumin seeds
1 tsp coriander seeds
1 tsp black peppercorns
½ tsp cloves
4 bay leaves
2 tsp smoked paprika

For the aromatic paste mix
1 onion, chopped
6 garlic cloves, peeled
2 red chillies, roughly
    chopped (seeds and all)
½ bunch of coriander
2 tbsp thyme leaves
2 tbsp rosemary leaves
Vegetable oil, for frying

For the sauce
200ml apple juice
100ml red wine vinegar
200ml tomato ketchup
100ml maple syrup
100g black treacle
2 tbsp Worcestershire sauce
2 tbsp Dijon mustard

To make the spice mix, heat a small frying pan over a medium-low heat and add all the spice seeds, peppercorns, cloves and bay leaves. Toast in the pan for a few minutes, shaking the pan from time to time, until fragrant; be careful not to scorch them. Remove from the heat and tip into a mortar. Allow to cool then bash together, crushing with the pestle to form a rough powder. Stir in the smoked paprika.

To make the aromatic paste mix, put the onion, garlic, chillies, coriander, thyme and rosemary into a food processor and whiz to a smooth paste. Heat a splash of oil in a medium-large saucepan over a low heat. Add the paste mix and cook, stirring frequently, over a medium-low heat for about 25–30 minutes, until softened and the paste is a nice golden brown. Stir in the toasted spice mix and cook for a further 2–3 minutes.

Pour in the apple juice and wine vinegar, whack up the heat and bring to the boil. Lower the heat and allow to bubble until reduced to half its original volume.

Next stir in the ketchup, maple syrup, treacle, Worcestershire sauce and mustard. Simmer very gently over a low heat for 15–20 minutes until the sauce has thickened and has a lovely, rich and glossy appearance. Remove from the heat and allow to cool, then whiz the sauce in a blender or food processor until smooth.

Pour into a sterilised cold glass jar or bottle, seal and refrigerate until needed. Use within a couple of weeks of making.

MUSHROOM KETCHUP

I like to smother steak and chicken in this rich and savoury sauce. It's also very good with Mediterranean chicken (page 83) and beef and beer loaf (page 102).
MAKES ABOUT 500ml

500g chestnut or portobello
   mushrooms
Vegetable oil, for frying
2 banana shallots, diced
100g demerara sugar
75ml white wine vinegar
400ml double cream
1 tsp salt
½ tsp cayenne pepper
¼ tsp smoked paprika
2 salted anchovies, chopped

Finely chop the mushrooms in a food processor using the pulse button – don't over-process to a purée. Alternatively, chop until very fine on a board with a knife.

Heat a large, non-stick frying pan or sauté pan over a medium-low heat and add a drizzle of oil. Add the shallots and cook for about 5–6 minutes, stirring from time to time, until softened.

Tip the mushrooms into the pan, turn up the heat and sweat for up to 10 minutes, stirring frequently, until a lot of their moisture has evaporated. They should be darkened and look quite dry.

Add the sugar and wine vinegar, stir to dissolve the sugar, and let bubble to reduce until the mushrooms are coated in a syrupy glaze. Stir in the cream, salt, cayenne pepper, smoked paprika and anchovies. Bring to the boil, then immediately lower the heat and reduce the sauce slowly by half.

Remove from the heat and allow to cool slightly, then transfer to a food processor or blender. Whiz until smooth, adding a trickle of water if necessary to loosen.

Pass the mixture through a fine sieve into a sterilised cold glass jar or bottle. Seal and refrigerate until needed. This ketchup will keep, sealed and refrigerated, for 4–5 days. Bring to room temperature before using, to enjoy it at its best.

Mushroom ketchup;
Tomato ketchup;
Spicy beetroot ketchup

TOMATO KETCHUP

I know it's hard to beat the market leader in this sauce, but it's always satisfying to make something yourself. I love this homemade version and I hope you will too. If you were my brother, you'd have it with everything, but I like it particularly with beef and beer loaf (page 102), pork and feta burgers (page 122), meatballs in chunky treacle gravy (page 106) and corn dogs (page 26). MAKES ABOUT 350ml

2 tbsp olive oil
2 celery sticks (tough strings
    removed with a vegetable
    peeler), finely chopped
1 small onion, chopped
1 garlic clove, finely grated
1 red chilli, chopped
    (seeds and all)
10 ripe plum tomatoes,
    roughly chopped
125g tomato purée
50g caster sugar
1 tsp salt
½ tsp ground mace
60ml cider vinegar
1 tbsp cornflour

Heat a large, non-stick frying pan over a medium-high heat and add the olive oil. Now add the celery, onion, garlic and chilli and cook for a few minutes to soften slightly. Stir in the tomatoes and continue to cook for 5–10 minutes, stirring frequently, until you have a rough, chunky sauce.

Transfer the mixture to a jug blender or food processor and whiz until smooth. Pass through a fine sieve into a bowl, pressing down with a spatula to extract as much of the sauce as possible.

Measure 350ml of the mixture into a large bowl. (Any excess can be used to dress pasta or spooned over deep-pan meat feast pizza, page 108.) Stir in the tomato purée, sugar, salt and mace then transfer to a saucepan. Return to the heat and cook for 4–5 minutes.

In a small bowl, mix together the cider vinegar and cornflour until smooth. Whisk this mixture into the tomato sauce and continue to cook over a low heat, stirring from time to time, for a further 15 minutes until thickened. Remove from the heat and allow to cool.

Once cooled, pass the sauce through the sieve again, directly into a jug. Finally, pour the ketchup into cold, sterilised jars or bottles and chill in the fridge until ready to use. It will keep, sealed in the fridge, for up to a month.

Illustrated on previous page

SPICY BEETROOT KETCHUP

This is a great alternative to tomato ketchup, with a similar richness of flavour to a good brown sauce. In fact, I use it in much the same way as brown sauce - with sausages, steak and cooked breakfasts. It's also fantastic with beef and beer loaf (page 102), marinated lamb ribs with roasted onions (page 96) and pulled pork shoulder (page 120). MAKES ABOUT 750ml

400g peeled, grated raw
   beetroot
200g peeled, grated raw
   carrot
250g cored, peeled, grated
   Bramley apple
50g grated garlic cloves
750ml water
60g balsamic vinegar
100g soft dark brown sugar
20g salt
½ tsp chilli powder
½ tsp ground ginger
½ tsp ground allspice
Salt and freshly ground
   black pepper

Put the beetroot, carrot, apple and garlic into a large saucepan. Pour in the water, then stir in the balsamic vinegar, sugar, salt, chilli powder, ground ginger and allspice.

Bring to the boil over a medium-high heat, then reduce the heat to a simmer and cook gently for 15–20 minutes, stirring from time to time, until all of the vegetables are soft and most of the liquid has evaporated. Remove from the heat and allow to cool slightly.

Transfer the mixture to a blender or food processor and whiz until smooth - you may need to do this in batches.

Pass through a sieve into a jug, pressing with a spatula to extract as much of the sauce as possible. Check the seasoning and add some salt and pepper if required.

Pour the ketchup into a sterilised glass jar or bottle. Seal and refrigerate until ready to use. It will keep for up to a week.

Illustrated on page 175

PUDDINGS

Who doesn't love a pudding? In Britain we famously have some of the world's finest. I've taken a selection of those old favourites and ramped them up a bit, so a basic bread and butter pudding becomes a nutty brioche pudding, speckled with chocolate and dried apricots. Similarly, inspired by the lovely custard tarts from my childhood, I've created individual little tarts that are a bit like the Portuguese *pasteis de nata*.

There are plenty of larger tarts too, because I think everyone should know how to throw one together. Whether you fancy a simple honey tart or something more elaborate, such as the peanut butter, cherry and chocolate one, with its lush combination of salty, sweet and silky, there's something to suit every mood and menu. The beauty of these tarts is that you can prepare them ahead – always a good thing if you want to spend more time with your family and friends than at the cooker.

For those who fancy more of a challenge, there are sophisticated whisky and rye puddings, which have a great depth of flavour and are not overwhelmingly sweet. Or there's my classic crème caramel, which I regard as foolproof. Or, for an easy treat, try the strawberry shortcakes – don't worry too much about making these look perfect, just put them together and dive right in!

In some ways, there's a bit of overlap here with the next chapter, Baking & Treats, as I like to think these puddings could be enjoyed at any time of the day. If you're like me, you don't always want a pudding after a big meal, but round about 11am or 4pm, and pretty much all points in between, you might feel the need for a boost that only a cup of coffee and something sweet can provide. So they're multi-purpose, user-friendly and infinitely adaptable... and I hope you'll give them a go.

NUTTY BRIOCHE PUDDING WITH CHOCOLATE

Creamy and comforting, bread and butter pudding is one of my all-time favourite puddings. This brioche version, which includes dried apricots, walnuts and chocolate, is especially luxurious, yet simple to make. SERVES 6–8

1 brioche loaf, about 500g, sliced (it can be slightly dry)

100g butter, softened, plus extra for greasing the dish

8 egg yolks

75g caster sugar

600ml double cream

1 tsp cardamom pods, lightly crushed

150g dried apricots, roughly chopped

150g shelled walnuts, toasted (see page 30) and chopped

150g dark chocolate (70% cocoa solids), broken into small pieces

Demerara sugar, for glazing

Lightly butter an ovenproof dish, about 23 x 33cm. Spread the brioche slices on both sides with the butter and set aside.

To make the custard, using an electric hand mixer, beat the egg yolks and sugar in a large bowl until the mixture becomes pale and fluffy. Meanwhile, put the cream and cardamom pods into a saucepan and place over a medium-high heat until bubbles start to appear around the edge of the pan.

Pour the cream through a sieve onto the egg and sugar mixture, whisking constantly. Pour the mixture back into a clean pan and return to a medium heat. Cook, stirring, for a few minutes until the custard thickens just enough to coat the back of a wooden spoon. Pass back through a fine sieve into a bowl or jug and let it cool slightly.

To assemble the pudding, pour a layer of custard into the greased dish. Scatter in half of the chopped apricots, walnuts and chocolate, then arrange a layer of buttered brioche on top. Repeat these layers, so you have two layers of brioche, then finish with a layer of custard. Leave to stand for 30 minutes (or refrigerate for up to 3–4 hours) before baking.

Preheat the oven to 140°C/Fan 120°C/Gas 1. Bake the pudding for 25–30 minutes until the custard is just set. Remove from the oven and leave to stand for 10 minutes.

Sprinkle a layer of demerara sugar on top of the pudding and glaze, using a cook's blowtorch, until caramelised and golden brown. If you don't have a blowtorch, place under a medium-hot grill for a couple of minutes until the sugar is caramelised. Serve with cream or ice cream if you fancy, though the pudding is very good just as it is.

WHISKY & RYE PUDDINGS

These sophisticated puddings are a cross between a rum baba and a baked doughnut. Soaked in boozy syrup, they taste utterly delicious, with a great balance of flavour from the rye breadcrumbs and the whisky. I like to serve them with crème Chantilly – whipped cream sweetened with a sprinkling of sugar and flavoured with a little vanilla extract. MAKES 6

For the puddings

70g butter, softened, plus extra for greasing

80g plain flour, plus extra for dusting

80g rice flour

40g dried rye breadcrumbs

½ tsp ground mace

A pinch of salt

7g sachet fast-action dried yeast

10g honey

4 medium-large eggs (250g total weight in shell), lightly beaten

For the whisky syrup

200ml water

200g caster sugar

75ml whisky

To serve

Crème chantilly (see above) or crème fraîche

Thin slivers cut from a vanilla pod (optional)

Lightly butter 6 savarin, dariole or timbale moulds, about 200ml capacity, then dust with flour and tap out any excess.

Put all of the pudding ingredients into a freestanding mixer fitted with the dough hook and combine on a medium-low speed for 5–10 minutes, to form a smooth, elastic dough.

Spoon the mixture into a piping bag fitted with a medium plain nozzle, or use a disposable piping bag with a 1cm hole cut at the end. Pipe the dough into the prepared moulds, cover loosely with cling film and leave to rise in a warm place for 45 minutes to 1 hour, until doubled in size.

Meanwhile, make the whisky syrup. Put the water and sugar in a saucepan and bring to the boil, stirring to dissolve the sugar. Boil for a couple of minutes until slightly thickened and syrupy, then take off the heat and stir in the whisky. Set aside.

When the puddings are almost ready, preheat the oven to 180°C/Fan 160°C/Gas 4. Remove the cling film and stand the moulds on a baking tray. Bake for 10–12 minutes until cooked through, golden and bouncy to the touch. Let cool in the tins.

Gently release the puddings from the moulds and place them in a deep dish (one in which the puddings just fit comfortably). Bring the whisky syrup back to the boil, then carefully pour over the puddings to submerge them. Cover the dish with cling film and leave the puddings to soak in the syrup for about 15 minutes, gently turning them a couple of times with a spoon so they absorb most of the syrup.

Serve the puddings warm or cold, with a little syrup spooned over and some crème chantilly or crème fraîche on top. Finish with slivers of vanilla pod, if you like.

SWEET SPICED CRÈME CARAMEL

This is my spiced-up crème caramel. It's always a winner and so simple to make. The key is to cook it very gently to make sure the custard doesn't split. Once you get that right, you'll go back to this recipe again and again, as a failsafe easy pud. SERVES 6–8

For the caramel
150g caster sugar

For the custard
600ml double cream
375ml condensed milk
2 tsp vanilla extract
1 tsp ground mace
½ tsp ground nutmeg
½ tsp ground cinnamon
8 eggs, plus 1 extra egg yolk
3 tbsp soft light brown sugar

Preheat the oven to 140°C/Fan 120°C/Gas 1. Have ready a round metal or ceramic pie dish, about 24cm in diameter and 5cm deep.

For the caramel, put the caster sugar and a splash of water into a large, stainless steel saucepan or deep sauté pan over a medium-high heat. Heat, stirring until the sugar dissolves.

Continue to heat the sugar syrup, swirling and shaking the pan rather than stirring to ensure even cooking, until it forms a light, coppery amber caramel. Immediately remove the pan from the heat to prevent the caramel from getting too dark and pour it directly into the pie dish. Set aside while you prepare the custard.

Put the cream, condensed milk, vanilla extract, mace, nutmeg and cinnamon into a large saucepan over a medium-high heat until bubbles start to appear around the edge of the pan, stirring a couple of times. Remove from the heat and set aside for a few minutes to let the flavours infuse.

Using a freestanding mixer fitted with the paddle attachment, or an electric hand mixer and large bowl, whisk together the whole eggs, egg yolk and sugar until the mixture is smooth, fluffy and thickened.

Strain the hot, spiced cream and milk mixture through a fine sieve onto the whisked mixture, whisking well to combine. Pour the mixture into a large jug and let it stand for a couple of minutes to settle and lose any air bubbles. Skim off any foam and carefully pour the custard on top of the caramel in the pie dish.

Stand the dish in a roasting tin and pour boiling water from the kettle into the tin until it comes halfway up the sides of the dish. Bake for about 40–50 minutes, until the custard has just set. Be careful not to overcook it – you want it to have a slight wobble to it when you gently shake the dish.

Remove from the oven and carefully lift the dish out of the water bath. Leave to cool, then cover with cling film and chill in the fridge for at least an hour before serving. (You can make this pudding a day or two before you want to serve it.)

To serve, gently release the crème caramel by running a small palette knife or table knife around the inside edge of the dish. Invert a large, lipped plate on top and carefully flip the dish and plate over, so the pudding sits on the plate and the golden caramel pours down the sides. Serve immediately.

RICH CHOCOLATE POTS WITH PORT RAISINS

These rich, decadent little puddings are so easy and you can prepare them a day ahead if you like. The port-soaked raisins are a great addition, but do experiment with other combinations too: try dried mango and rum, prunes and brandy, or even dried apricots and cider – they all work brilliantly. SERVES 8

For the raisins
100g raisins
100ml ruby port

For the chocolate pots
200g dark chocolate (about 70% cocoa solids), chopped into very small pieces
400ml double cream
1 vanilla pod, split in half lengthways
5 egg yolks
80g dark muscovado sugar
A pinch of flaky sea salt
100g crème fraîche, stirred until smooth

Put the raisins into a small, heatproof bowl. In a small pan, bring the port to the boil. Pour it over the raisins, cover and leave them to soak up the liquid for at least 30 minutes (or up to 4 hours). Drain the raisins of any excess port.

To make the chocolate pots, put the chocolate into a medium heatproof bowl. Pour the cream into a saucepan. Using the point of a small, sharp knife, scrape out the seeds from the vanilla pod directly into the cream and add the pod too. Place over a medium heat until bubbles start to appear around the edge of the pan.

While the cream is heating, using an electric hand mixer, whisk the egg yolks and sugar together in a bowl until the mixture is light and fluffy. Remove the vanilla pod from the pan, then slowly pour the hot cream onto the eggs and sugar, whisking all the time. Pour the mixture back into a clean saucepan and heat gently, stirring constantly, until thickened enough to coat the back of a wooden spoon.

Pass this custard through a fine sieve onto the chocolate. Let it stand for a couple of minutes or so until the chocolate starts to melt, then add the sea salt and stir until smooth. Allow to cool, then stir in the crème fraîche.

Divide the raisins between 8 ramekins or other small dishes, 125ml capacity. Spoon or pipe the chocolate custard into the dishes – it's easier to get a neat result with a piping bag. Cover with cling film and leave to set in the fridge for at least 2 hours.

Take the puddings out of the fridge 20 minutes before serving. Sprinkle with a little flaky salt, if you like, as you serve them.

BUTTERNUT SQUASH TART

In my version of pumpkin pie, I use butternut squash because it has a silky texture and a lower water content than other pumpkins. If you can, prepare the squash a day ahead, to allow plenty of time to drain off the excess liquid. Alternatively, you can use a tin of solid-pack pumpkin – just make sure it is not seasoned. SERVES 8–10

For the pastry
220g plain flour, plus extra
    for dusting
140g butter, chilled and diced
½ tsp salt
75ml iced water
Juice of ½ lemon
1 egg, lightly beaten

For the filling
2 butternut squash, about
    500g each (or a 400g tin
    of solid-pack pumpkin)
A pinch of salt
4 eggs
120g soft light brown sugar
1 tsp ground ginger
½ tsp ground cinnamon
½ tsp freshly ground nutmeg
125ml maple syrup
350ml double cream

To make the pastry, put the flour, butter and salt into a food processor and pulse until the mixture resembles breadcrumbs. (Alternatively, you can do this in a bowl, rubbing the butter in with your fingertips.) Add the water and lemon juice and bring the dough together with your hands.

Remove the pastry from the bowl, wrap in cling film and leave to rest in the fridge for at least an hour, or overnight.

Preheat the oven to 180°C/Fan 160°C/Gas 4.

Roll out the pastry on a lightly floured surface to the thickness of a £1 coin. Use to line a 25cm loose-bottomed tart tin, gently pressing the pastry into the base and sides and allowing any excess to hang over the edges of the tin.

Stand the tart tin on a baking sheet. Line the pastry case with baking parchment and fill with ceramic baking beans, dried pulses or uncooked rice. Bake 'blind' for 20–25 minutes, then remove from the oven and lift out the parchment and baking beans. Bake for a further 10 minutes until the pastry is evenly golden brown all over.

Brush the base of the tart with beaten egg and return to the oven for a further 2 minutes to help seal the pastry. Let cool, then trim away the excess pastry with a small, serrated knife.

For the filling, halve, peel and deseed the squash, then cut the flesh into 3cm chunks. Place in a foil-lined roasting tin, season very lightly with salt and add a small splash of water. Cover with a second sheet of foil and scrunch the edges together to make a parcel, sealing it well. Bake for about an hour, until the squash is very tender. Tear open the foil and leave the squash to cool. Lower the oven setting to 170°C/Fan 150°C/Gas 3½.

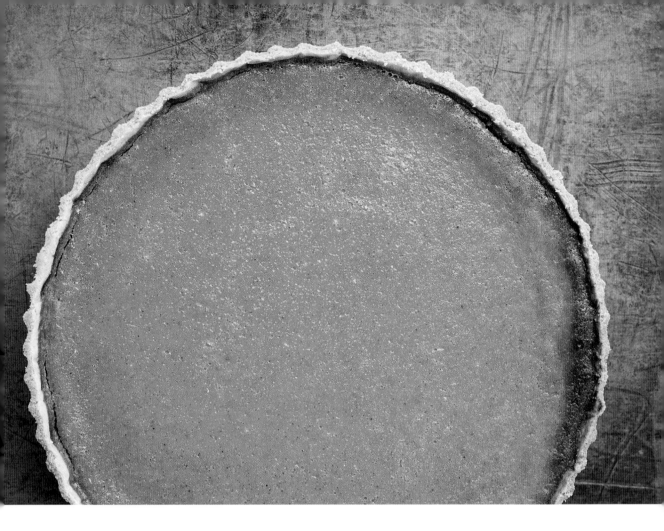

Transfer the cooled squash to a food processor and blitz to a silky smooth purée. Pass through a fine sieve. (If it's at all watery, tip into a muslin-lined colander and leave to drain off the excess liquid, preferably overnight but at least for a few hours, then squeeze well.) Weigh out 400g pulp for the filling; any excess squash purée can be frozen for another use.

Using a freestanding mixer fitted with the beater attachment, or an electric hand mixer and large bowl, whisk the eggs and sugar together until the mixture is light, creamy and aerated. Add the ginger, cinnamon, nutmeg and maple syrup and beat well to combine. Add the squash along with the cream and beat for a minute or two, until the mixture is very smooth.

Pour into the pastry case and bake for 40–50 minutes, until the filling is just set, with a slight wobble in the centre. Take out of the oven and leave to cool. Release the tart from the tin and cut into slices. Serve with soured cream or crème fraîche.

PECAN TART

Pecans have a rich flavour and a great texture, particularly if you toast them, but you can make this tart with walnuts instead if you prefer. Whatever nuts you use, a sprinkling of flaky sea salt at the end really lifts the flavours. Serve a slice just as it is with a cup of coffee or tea, or with a scoop of good vanilla ice cream as an indulgent dessert. SERVES 8–10

For the sweet pastry
250g butter, softened
120g caster sugar
400g plain flour, plus extra
    for dusting
1 egg, lightly beaten

For the filling
500g shelled pecans nuts
3 eggs
180g caster sugar
1 tsp ground mace
50ml golden syrup
50ml black treacle
50g butter, melted
1 tsp salt
2 vanilla pods, split in half
    lengthways and seeds
    scraped out
50ml whisky or dark rum

To finish
Flaky sea salt

To make the pastry, using a freestanding mixer fitted with the beater attachment or an electric hand mixer and large bowl, cream together the butter and sugar until smooth and pale. Reduce the speed and slowly add the flour. Just before it's fully combined, add the egg and mix briefly, just until smooth.

Remove the pastry from the bowl, wrap in cling film and leave to rest in the fridge for at least 1 hour, or overnight.

Preheat the oven to 180°C/Fan 160°C/Gas 4.

Roll out the pastry on a lightly floured surface to the thickness of a £1 coin. Use to line a 28cm loose-bottomed tart tin, about 4cm deep, gently pressing the pastry into the base and sides and allowing any excess to hang over the edges of the tin.

Stand the tart tin on a baking sheet. Line the pastry case with baking parchment and fill with ceramic baking beans, dried pulses or uncooked rice. Bake 'blind' for 20–25 minutes, then remove from the oven and lift out the parchment and baking beans. Bake for a further 10–15 minutes, until the pastry is evenly golden brown all over. Leave to cool, then trim away the excess pastry with a small, serrated knife.

For the filling, scatter the pecans on a large baking tray and place in the oven at 180°C/Fan 160°C/Gas 4 until fragrant and lightly toasted, about 5–7 minutes. Leave to cool.

Put half the toasted pecans in a food processor and pulse to crush lightly. Continue to pulse further if you'd like a finer-textured filling. Alternatively, place the nuts in a self-sealing plastic bag and bash with a rolling pin until you achieve the texture you like.

Using a freestanding mixer fitted with the whisk attachment, or a hand mixer with a whisk attachment, whisk together the eggs, sugar and mace until pale, light and fluffy. Add the golden syrup, treacle, melted butter, salt, vanilla seeds and whisky or rum and whisk until incorporated. Now use a spatula to fold in the blitzed pecans until evenly combined.

Pour the pecan filling into the pastry case. Arrange the whole pecans decoratively on top. Bake the tart for 25–30 minutes until it's evenly coloured, lightly golden brown and almost set – it should still have a slight wobble in the centre when you gently shake the tin.

Remove from the oven and leave the tart to rest for about an hour before serving. Don't be tempted to serve it too early as the filling needs to cool and set, to stop it being runny when you cut into it. Once cool, sprinkle with flaky sea salt. Serve as it is, or with scoops of good vanilla ice cream, if you like.

HONEY TART

This tart has a fantastically rich, subtle flavour with a seductively silky texture. You only need a small slice, as a little goes a long way. If I can, I like to use a good local honey in this recipe. It's an excellent way to enjoy the unique and distinctive flavour. Source one from a farm shop or local market if you can, otherwise use a good quality supermarket honey. SERVES 8–10

For the sweet pastry
170g butter, softened
80g caster sugar
270g plain flour, plus extra
    for dusting
1 egg, lightly beaten

For the filling
5 eggs
1 vanilla pod, split in half
    lengthways and seeds
    scraped out
A pinch of salt
250g soft light brown sugar
100ml double cream
85g honey
70g butter
65ml white wine vinegar
2 tbsp golden syrup
50g fine polenta

To finish
Edible flowers, such as
    violas, or a pinch of
    flaky sea salt

To make the pastry, using a freestanding mixer fitted with the beater attachment or an electric hand mixer and large bowl, cream together the butter and sugar on a medium-high speed until the mixture is smooth and pale. Reduce the speed and slowly add the flour. Just before it is fully incorporated, add enough egg to bring the dough together (you won't need all of it) and mix briefly, just until smooth.

Remove the pastry from the bowl and wrap it in cling film. Place it in the fridge to rest for at least 1 hour, or overnight if that's more convenient.

Preheat the oven to 180°C/Fan 160°C/Gas 4.

As the pastry is fragile and a bit tricky to handle you'll find it easier to roll out between 2 sheets of cling film. Roll it out to the thickness of a £1 coin and use to line a loose-bottomed oblong tart tin, about 36 x 12cm, or a 25cm round tart tin, about 3cm deep. The easiest way to do this is to peel off the top layer of cling film and invert the pastry into the tin, then remove the other layer of cling film. Gently press the pastry into the base and sides of the tin and allow any excess to hang over the edges of the tin.

Stand the tart tin on a baking sheet. Line the pastry case with baking parchment and fill with ceramic baking beans, dried pulses or uncooked rice. Bake 'blind' for 20–25 minutes, then remove from the oven and lift out the parchment and baking beans. Bake for a further 10–15 minutes, until the pastry is evenly golden brown all over. Leave to cool, then trim away the excess pastry with a small, serrated knife.

Lower the oven temperature to 170°C/Fan 150°C/Gas 3½.

To make the filling, whisk the eggs, vanilla seeds and salt together in a large bowl until combined.

Put the sugar, cream, honey, butter, wine vinegar and golden syrup into a medium-large saucepan over a medium-high heat and bring to the boil, stirring.

Remove from the heat and slowly stir in the polenta and the egg mixture. Return to a very low heat and cook, stirring constantly, for about 5 minutes until smooth; don't let the mixture boil or it will curdle. Transfer to a large jug and allow it to sit for a few minutes.

Pour the filling into the pastry case. Bake for 20 minutes, or until the filling is evenly coloured and just set – it should have a slight wobble in the centre when you gently shake the tin.

Leave to cool, then carefully remove the tart from the tin and place on a board or serving plate. Decorate with edible flowers or finish with a sprinkling of flaky sea salt.

Cut the honey tart into slices and serve with clotted cream or good vanilla ice cream.

Illustrated overleaf

PEANUT BUTTER, CHERRY & CHOCOLATE TART

Layers of great flavours are the key to this fantastic tart. There's very little cooking required, but it does take a little time for the layers to set so you will need to be patient – I promise you it's worth the wait! SERVES 12–16

For the base
50g shelled hazelnuts
150g digestive biscuits
50g butter, melted, plus extra
    for greasing the tin

For the filling
200g smooth peanut butter
    (at room temperature)
40g caster sugar
A pinch of salt
50g butter, melted

For the jam layer
250g black cherry jam

For the chocolate ganache
300g dark chocolate
    (70% cocoa solids),
    very finely chopped
300ml double cream
25ml sesame oil

Preheat the oven to 180°C/Fan 160°C/Gas 4. Lightly grease a 23cm loose-bottomed shallow round cake tin with butter and line the base and sides with non-stick baking parchment.

For the base, scatter the hazelnuts on a baking sheet and roast in the oven for 10–12 minutes, until the skins are blistered. Wrap in a clean tea towel and let them steam for a couple of minutes then rub in the tea towel to remove the skins (as much you can).

Turn the oven up to 200°C/Fan 180°C/Gas 6.

To make the base, whiz the hazelnuts in a food processor until coarsely ground; don't over-process or they will become oily. Add the biscuits and blitz to a fine powder. Now pour in the melted butter and blitz for a few more seconds to combine.

Tip the biscuit mixture into the prepared cake tin and use a spoon to press and level it out. Bake for 10 minutes until set, then remove from the oven and leave to cool in the tin.

Meanwhile, make the filling. Using an electric hand whisk and large bowl or a freestanding mixer fitted with the whisk attachment, whip the peanut butter, sugar and salt together until the mixture is soft, light and nicely aerated. Pour in the melted butter and whisk again briefly, to combine.

Pour the filling over the cooled biscuit base and spread it out evenly, being careful not to break the biscuit layer. Cover with cling film and chill in the fridge for about 2 hours until firm.

Spread the cherry jam over the set peanut butter filling, cover with cling film and return to the fridge for at least 15 minutes.

At this stage you can leave it for several hours, even overnight if that's more convenient.

For the ganache, put the chocolate into a large, heatproof bowl. Pour the cream into a pan, add the sesame oil and heat until bubbles appear around the edge of the pan. Immediately pour onto the chocolate and leave to stand for 2 minutes. Stir with a spatula just until smooth, glossy and shiny – no longer.

Pour the chocolate ganache over the surface of the tart, spreading it evenly over the jam layer with a spatula or the back of a spoon. Cover with cling film and return to the fridge to set for at least 2 hours, or overnight.

When you're ready to serve, remove the tart from the tin and cut it into slices – it's very rich, so a thin sliver per serving is usually enough. Serve with whipped cream or crème fraîche, if you like.

CUSTARD TARTS

Custard tarts are such a classic from my childhood. Made with puff pastry, these individual tarts are very easy. They look rustic – like traditional Portuguese tarts – and have a delicate, crispy case and velvety soft filling. If you can, serve them warm when they're absolutely delicious, but they're great cold too. MAKES 12–14

Butter, for greasing
Plain flour, for dusting
500g ready-made all-butter
    puff pastry

For the custard
375ml whole milk
150g caster sugar
2 vanilla pods, split in half
    lengthways and seeds
    scraped out
1 tbsp cornflour
90ml evaporated milk
4 eggs, plus 4 extra egg yolks
Freshly grated nutmeg

Preheat the oven to 180°C/Fan 160°C/Gas 4.

Grease 14 deep-fill foil mince pie tart cases with a little butter. Dust each one with a good sprinkling of flour, shake out any excess and set aside. (If you can't find foil cases, use 2 large, 12-hole muffin tins, greasing only 14 of the moulds.)

Roll out the pastry on a lightly floured surface to roughly the thickness of a £1 coin. Using a suitably sized saucer as a template, cut out 12–14 circles, making sure they are big enough to comfortably line the foil cases.

Gently press the pastry into the foil cases (or moulds), making sure it sits snugly on the base and sides. Allow the pastry to overlap the top of the moulds just slightly, to allow for any shrinkage. (You can trim away any excess after baking.)

If you're using foil pastry cases, place them on a couple of baking sheets. Bake the pastry cases for 20–25 minutes, until the pastry is evenly coloured, golden brown and just crisp. Remove from the oven and allow to cool.

Lower the oven temperature to 150°C/Fan 130°C/Gas 2.

While the tart cases are cooling, make the custard. Heat the milk, sugar and vanilla seeds in a medium-large saucepan over a medium heat, stirring occasionally, until bubbles start to appear around the edge of the pan. Take off the heat.

Put the cornflour into a large bowl, add a splash of evaporated milk and whisk together to make a smooth paste. Pour in the rest of the evaporated milk and whisk until it is fully incorporated. Add the eggs and egg yolks to the bowl and beat together until evenly combined.

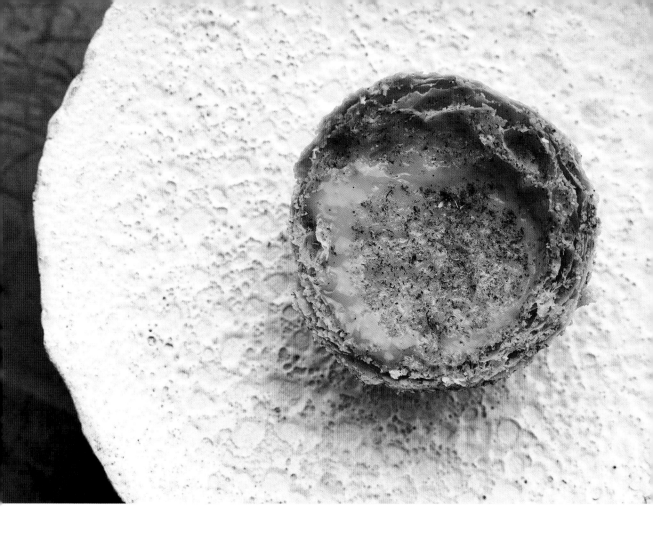

Now pour on the hot milk mixture, whisking constantly. Return to the pan and heat gently, stirring, until thickened enough to coat the back of a wooden spoon. Pass through a fine sieve into a jug. Let the custard sit for a few minutes to settle any air bubbles, then skim the top to remove any foam.

When the tart cases are cold, trim off the excess pastry from the edges. Gently hollow out the tart cases slightly, removing some of the pastry to make room for the custard filling.

Carefully pour the custard into the tart cases, to reach almost to the top, then dust generously with grated nutmeg. Bake for 10–15 minutes, until the custard is set but still has a slight wobble to it when you gently shake the cases (or tins). Make sure you do not overcook the custard.

Remove the tarts from the oven and leave to stand for about 5 minutes before serving. They're lovely eaten while still warm.

STRAWBERRY SHORTCAKES & MASCARPONE CREAM

These luscious little shortcakes are a gorgeous, informal way to end a summer party, when strawberries are ripe, plentiful and cheap. I don't worry about how these look – if they're a bit messy, who cares? They taste amazing. MAKES ABOUT 16

For the shortcakes
300g plain flour, plus extra
    for dusting
50g caster sugar
1 tbsp baking powder
½ tsp salt
225g butter, chilled and
    diced
1 egg, lightly beaten
150ml whole milk

For the strawberries
600g ripe strawberries
3 tbsp caster sugar
2 tbsp chopped mint leaves

For the mascarpone cream
100g mascarpone cheese
100ml double cream
35g caster sugar
¼–½ tsp cracked black
    pepper

To serve
Icing sugar, for dusting
    (optional)

To make the shortcakes, put the flour, sugar, baking powder and salt into a large bowl and stir to combine. Add the butter and use your fingertips to rub everything together, lightly working the mixture until it resembles fine breadcrumbs.

In a small, separate bowl, mix the egg and milk together. Stir into the rubbed-in mixture to create a smooth, soft dough. Knead very briefly, bringing the dough together to form a ball – the secret to a tender shortcake is working as quickly and lightly as possible. Wrap the dough in cling film and chill in the fridge for an hour.

Preheat the oven to 200°C/Fan 180°C/Gas 6. Line one or two baking trays with non-stick baking parchment.

Roll out the dough on a lightly floured surface to a 1.5cm thickness. Using a 5cm round pastry cutter dipped in flour, stamp out 16 shortcakes from the dough. (Don't gather up and roll out the pastry trimmings, as they will be tough.)

Carefully place the shortbread rounds on the prepared baking tray(s) and bake for 12-15 minutes, until lightly golden and crisp. Remove from the oven and leave to cool on the tray(s) for a few minutes, then transfer them to a wire rack and leave to cool completely.

Meanwhile, prepare the strawberries. Quarter or slice them and place in a bowl. Sprinkle over the sugar and mix gently, just to coat the strawberries evenly. Leave to macerate for at least 30 minutes – the sugar will soften the strawberries and bring out their juices, allowing them to steep in their liquid. Just before serving, toss through the chopped mint.

For the mascarpone cream, put the mascarpone, cream and sugar in a bowl and whip together, using an electric hand mixer with a whisk attachment, until smooth and holding peaks – be careful not to overbeat it. Fold in ¼ tsp of the cracked pepper, taste and add a little more pepper if you like.

Place the shortcakes on serving plates, pile the strawberries on them and then add dollops of the mascarpone cream. Finish with a trickle of the strawberry juices, and a dusting of icing sugar, if you like.

BLACK GRAPE, MINT & MERINGUE TART

I never understand why we don't cook with grapes more often. We might use them as a garnish for a cheese plate, but we're seldom more adventurous than that. But they contain so much lovely natural juice and have such a great balance of sweetness and acidity, they're up there as my favourite fruit – this tart is my celebration of that.
SERVES 8–12

For the sweet pastry
250g butter, softened
120g caster sugar
400g plain flour, plus extra
    for dusting
1 egg, lightly beaten

For the filling
1.2kg seedless black grapes
50g caster sugar
30g cornflour
Juice of 1 lemon
4 tbsp chopped mint leaves

For the meringue topping
150g egg whites (about
    4 large whites)
300g caster sugar
70ml water
25g glucose syrup

To make the pastry, using a freestanding mixer fitted with the beater attachment or an electric hand mixer and large bowl, cream together the butter and sugar on a medium-high speed until the mixture is smooth and pale. Reduce the speed and slowly add the flour. Just before it's fully combined, add the egg and mix briefly just until smooth.

Remove from the bowl, wrap in cling film and refrigerate for at least 1 hour, or overnight.

Preheat the oven to 180°C/Fan 160°C/Gas 4.

Roll out the pastry on a lightly floured surface to the thickness of a £1 coin. Use to line a 25cm loose-bottomed tart tin, about 4cm deep, gently pressing the pastry into the base and sides and allowing any excess to hang over the edges of the tin.

Stand the tart tin on a baking sheet. Line the pastry case with baking parchment and fill with ceramic baking beans, dried pulses or uncooked rice. Bake 'blind' for 20–25 minutes, then remove from the oven and lift out the parchment and baking beans. Bake for a further 10–15 minutes, until the pastry is evenly golden brown all over. Leave to cool, then trim away the excess pastry with a small, serrated knife.

Next prepare the filling. Cut half of the grapes in two and place them in a large saucepan over a very low heat with the sugar. Poach gently for around 10 minutes, stirring from time to time, so the grapes steep in their own juices but still retain some of their shape.

In a small bowl, mix together the cornflour and lemon juice to form a paste. Whisk this into the grape juice in the pan and continue to heat very gently for 1–2 minutes, until the mixture thickens. Remove from the heat and leave to cool.

When the grape filling is almost cold, stir in the chopped mint. Once cooled completely, stir in the whole grapes. Spoon into the cooked pastry case and spread out evenly with a spoon.

Next make the meringue. Make sure all of your equipment is scrupulously clean. Using a stand mixer or electric hand mixer, whisk the egg whites on a medium-high speed until they form soft peaks. Set aside briefly while you make the hot sugar syrup.

Put the sugar, water and glucose syrup into a saucepan over a medium heat, stirring to dissolve the sugar. Bring to the boil and heat until it registers 118°C on a cook's thermometer, i.e. the 'soft ball' stage. (If you don't have a thermometer, to test, drop a small amount of the syrup into a glass of cold water: it should form a soft ball.) With the mixer running, slowly pour the hot syrup onto the egg whites and continue whisking until the meringue is cool. It will be incredibly glossy, shiny and have reached firm peaks by this stage.

Spoon, spread or pipe the meringue on top of the grapes in the tart tin. It's up to you how you decorate it – give it some height, swirls and peaks. Leave to set for 30 minutes.

Using a cook's blowtorch, carefully caramelise the surface of the tart until the meringue is lightly coloured. If you don't have a blowtorch, place the tart under a medium-hot grill for a minute or two to colour – keep a close eye on it, as the meringue can quickly burn.

Serve immediately, cut into slices using a serrated knife.

Illustrated overleaf

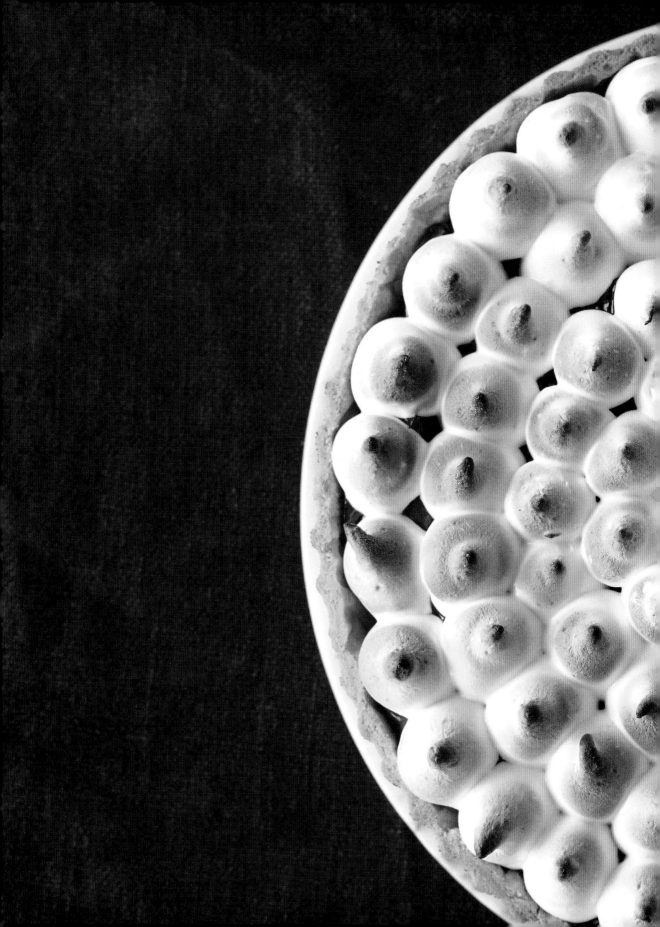

BLITZ TORTE

This gorgeous German concoction is part cake, part meringue and part custard, with a bit of fruit thrown in for good measure. What more can you ask for from a pud? I use strawberries here, but you can change the fruit to match the seasons or your tastes – tropical fruits work particularly well. SERVES 8–10

For the cake

120g butter, plus extra for greasing

70g caster sugar

4 egg yolks (save the whites for the meringue, below)

1 tsp vanilla extract

140g plain flour

1 tsp baking powder

3 tbsp whole milk

For the meringue

4 egg whites

¼ tsp cream of tartar

130g caster sugar

1 tsp white wine vinegar

100g slivered almonds

For the custard filling

4 egg yolks

130g caster sugar

3 tbsp plain flour

1 vanilla pod, split in half lengthways and seeds scraped out

300ml double cream

200g strawberries, very large ones halved

To finish

Icing sugar, for dusting

Preheat the oven to 160°C/Fan 140°C/Gas 3. Lightly grease the base and sides of two 24cm square loose-bottomed cake tins with butter and line the bases with non-stick baking parchment. If you don't have loose-bottomed square tins, use ordinary tins and let the parchment overhang the sides a bit, to make it easier to remove the cakes.

For the cake batter, using a freestanding mixer fitted with the beater attachment, or an electric hand mixer and bowl, beat the butter and sugar together on a medium-low speed until the mixture is light, pale and fluffy. Add the egg yolks and vanilla extract and mix together briefly to combine.

In a separate bowl, sift together the flour and baking powder. On a low speed, add the flour mixture to the butter and sugar a little at a time, beating just enough to combine; do not overwork. Add the milk to loosen the mixture a little. Divide the batter between the prepared cake tins and set aside.

Next make the meringue. Make sure all of your equipment is scrupulously clean. Using the mixer, whisk the egg whites on a medium-high speed until they form soft peaks. With the machine running, add the cream of tartar, then the sugar, a spoonful at a time, whisking until the mixture forms stiff, glossy peaks. Add the vinegar and whisk briefly to incorporate.

Using a spatula, spread half of the meringue over the batter in one of the cake tins. Using a piping bag fitted with a large nozzle, pipe the meringue on top of the batter in the other tin and sprinkle with the almonds – this will be the top layer.

Bake the cakes for 30–35 minutes, until the meringue is set and lightly golden. Leave to cool in the tins for 10 minutes, then carefully transfer to a wire rack to cool completely.

Meanwhile, make the custard filling. Using an electric hand mixer fitted with the whisk attachment, beat the egg yolks and sugar together in a large heatproof bowl until the mixture is pale and fluffy. Fold in the flour and vanilla seeds. Pour in the cream and whisk to combine.

Now place the bowl over of a pan of barely simmering water, making sure the water doesn't touch the bowl, and whisk constantly until the custard thickens. This could take as long as 15–20 minutes; don't let it boil or it may curdle. Once it is the consistency of thick custard, remove the bowl from the heat and leave to cool completely. As the custard cools, it will thicken a bit more.

To assemble the cake, spread the custard on top of the plain meringue cake. Arrange the strawberries in rows on top and gently press them right down into the custard. Position the decorated meringue cake on top, with the almonds uppermost. Dust the cake with icing sugar and cut into slices to serve.

BAKED VANILLA CHEESECAKE

Baked cheesecakes have a rich and creamy texture and are more satisfying than their uncooked counterparts. Serve this classic baked cheesecake with ripe berries in summer, or a spiced fruit compote in winter. It really is a pud for all seasons, so feel free to adapt it as you like. SERVES 10–12

For the base
225g digestive biscuits
40g caster sugar
100g butter, melted, plus
    extra for greasing

For the filling
750g soft full-fat cream
    cheese, such as
    Philadelphia
400g crème fraîche
170g caster sugar
45g plain flour
A pinch of salt
2 vanilla pod(s), split in
    half lengthways and
    seeds scraped out
Finely grated zest and juice
    of 1 unwaxed lime
6 large egg yolks

To serve (optional)
Seasonal fruit

Preheat the oven to 180°C/Fan 160°C/Gas 4.

Lightly grease the base and sides of a 23cm round springform cake tin with butter and line with non-stick baking parchment. Butter the parchment.

To make the base, put the biscuits into a food processor and whiz to crumbs. Alternatively, place them in a self-sealing plastic bag and bash with a rolling pin until finely crushed. Tip the crumbs into a large bowl and stir in the sugar. Add the melted butter and mix to combine.

Tip the crumb mixture into the prepared cake tin, spread evenly and press down firmly with the back of a spoon so the base is nice and compact. Bake for 10–15 minutes. Remove from the oven and leave to cool completely in the tin.

Meanwhile, prepare the filling. Using either a freestanding mixer fitted with the whisk attachment or an electric hand mixer and bowl, beat the cream cheese, crème fraîche and sugar together on a medium speed for a couple of minutes until the mixture is very smooth and creamy.

Sift the flour and salt over the mixture and mix again briefly, just to combine. Add the vanilla seeds, lime zest and juice, and whisk slowly, until evenly blended. Now incorporate the egg yolks, one at a time, beating briefly after each addition and scraping the bowl down as necessary with a spatula. Do not overbeat – you want the filling to be smooth, light and aerated.

Pour the filling on top of the biscuit base, gently levelling out the surface with a spoon or a palette knife. Give the tin a

gentle tap on a flat surface to ensure there are no air pockets in the mixture, and stand the tin on a baking sheet.

Bake at 180°C/160°C Fan/Gas 4 for 10 minutes, then turn the oven down to 140°C/Fan 120°C/Gas 1 and bake for a further 1 hour and 10 minutes. The filling should be set but have a slight wobble in the centre when you gently shake the tin. Do not overcook, as it will firm up considerably as it cools.

Turn off the oven and prop the oven door open slightly. Leave the cheesecake inside to 'rest' for around 15–20 minutes, then remove from the oven and leave to stand at room temperature for at least 3 hours. It's now ready to serve, but can be chilled if you're not eating it straight away.

To unmould the cheesecake, run a knife around the edge of the tin, removing the parchment, and transfer the cheesecake to a plate. Cut into wedges and serve just as it is, or with fruit.

BAKING
& TREATS

For lots of us, baking was our first experience of cooking, either at home or at school. Few things can touch that sense of pride at our first batch of biscuits or rock buns, even if they weren't all that brilliant to look at. I'd like to think we can keep hold of that sense of cheerfulness and not get too hung up on perfection. At its best, baking is a science, but even if your efforts are a bit wobbly around the edges, they will invariably taste much better than most things you can buy.

I've included a cornbread and an easy oat and sunflower seed bread, because it's always good to be able to throw together something to go with soup or salad. Otherwise, most of the recipes in this chapter are sweet. Whether you want to start the day with some blueberry muffins or end it with a bowl or mug of continental hot chocolate, I hope you'll find several recipes to tempt you here.

I always like to include something a little unexpected to keep us all on our toes! For example, I stud my rocky road with flecks of red chilli and tangy dried mango, which adds interest. My blondies are given a rich and sophisticated edge with the addition of sesame oil and seeds, and my carrot cake has a luscious mascarpone and coconut icing.

And I like to have a bit of fun too. Step forward, popcorn bars, which are some of the easiest things you could possibly make and seem to be a big hit with everyone, whether they're eight or eighty. They're a great reminder that whatever you're cooking, whatever the occasion, it should taste good and most definitely make you smile.

OAT & SUNFLOWER SEED BREAD

This bread has a substantial, wholesome texture with a nice bite from the sunflower seeds and a touch of sweetness from the honey but it isn't at all heavy. I like it particularly with a good Cheddar cheese, or toasted for breakfast. There's enough here for two loaves – if you don't think you are likely to eat both before they lose their freshness, pop one in the freezer for later. MAKES 2 LOAVES

390g strong white bread flour, plus extra for dusting

1 tbsp caster sugar

2 x 7g sachets fast-action dried yeast

450ml warm water

280g wholemeal flour

140g rolled oats

75g butter, softened, plus extra for greasing

75g honey

45g dried milk powder

2 tsp salt

135g sunflower seeds

Vegetable oil, for oiling

Grease two 1kg loaf tins with a little butter and line the bases and sides with non-stick baking parchment.

Make the bread in a freestanding electric mixer fitted with the dough hook. Put the white flour, sugar and yeast into the bowl and start mixing on a medium-low speed. With the motor running, gradually add the warm water. Continue to knead in the mixer for around 10 minutes until the dough is smooth, silky and elastic.

Add the wholemeal flour, oats, softened butter, honey, milk powder and salt and continue to mix for a couple more minutes until everything is well combined. Sprinkle the sunflower seeds into the bowl and mix briefly to combine.

Lightly oil a large bowl, place the dough in the bowl and cover with cling film. Leave to rise in a warm place for about an hour, until it is doubled in size, and light and springy to the touch.

Turn the dough out onto a lightly floured surface and knock back briefly by gently kneading with your hands. Don't overdo this or you may lose the lightness of the bread – you're just looking to remove any large air pockets. Once it's knocked back, divide the dough in half.

Mould and shape the dough into the prepared loaf tins, pressing them in gently. Cover each loosely with cling film. Leave to prove in a warm place for a further 45 minutes to 1 hour until the loaves are doubled in size.

Meanwhile, preheat the oven to 210°C/Fan 190°C/Gas 7.

Uncover the loaves and bake for 45–50 minutes until golden brown and cooked through. If you remove one of the loaves from its tin, it should feel firm and sound a little hollow when you tap it on the bottom.

Leave the loaves to cool in the tins for 5–10 minutes, then turn out and place on a wire rack. Remove the parchment and let the loaves cool completely before slicing to serve.

CORNBREAD

Cornbread is so simple to make and it's great with soups, stews, salads and chillies. Try it with venison chilli (page 116) or green chilli con carne (page 118) and you'll see what I mean. It's normally eaten as a savoury bread, but it does work surprisingly well toasted and served with any red fruit jam. MAKES 12 SQUARES

A knob of butter, for greasing
Caster sugar, for dusting
200g plain flour
200g fine polenta
2 tsp baking powder
1 tsp bicarbonate of soda
½ tsp salt
½ tsp cracked black pepper
400ml buttermilk
2 eggs, lightly beaten
75g butter, melted and
    cooled slightly
170g cooked sweetcorn
    kernels, well drained

Preheat the oven to 190°C/Fan 170°C/Gas 5.

Lightly butter a 20cm square loose-bottomed cake tin and sprinkle with sugar, shaking out any excess. (Or grease and line a solid 20cm square tin with non-stick baking parchment, letting some overhang the sides to make it easier to lift out the cornbread later. Butter and sugar the parchment.)

In a large bowl, mix together the flour, polenta, baking powder, bicarbonate of soda, salt and pepper until well combined.

In a separate, smaller bowl, whisk the buttermilk and eggs together until combined. Add to the flour mixture along with the melted butter and stir to combine, creating a smooth batter. Finally, fold in the sweetcorn.

Pour the mixture into the prepared cake tin and bake for 45–50 minutes, until lightly golden and springy to the touch. A skewer inserted into the middle should come out clean.

Leave the cornbread to cool in the tin for up to 10 minutes, then turn out and place on a wire rack to cool completely.

Cut the cornbread into squares to serve. It is best eaten as soon as possible after it is made, though slightly older cornbread is still good toasted.

VANILLA & CORN BAKE

I know this sounds like an unlikely combination, but it's suprisingly good. Topped with a trickle of golden syrup or maple syrup it makes a lovely pudding, or you can serve it as a brunch with a few rashers of crisp streaky bacon on the side. SERVES 8

A little butter, softened,
    for greasing
300ml whole milk
300ml double cream
200ml evaporated milk
2 vanilla pods, split in half
    lengthways
3 eggs, separated, plus
    3 extra egg yolks
50g soft light brown sugar
50g plain flour
100g caster sugar
500g cooked sweetcorn
    kernels, well drained
1 tsp baking powder
½ tsp salt

To serve
Golden syrup or maple
    syrup, to trickle
Vanilla ice cream, double
    cream or crème fraîche
    (optional)

Preheat the oven to 180°C/Fan 160°C/Gas 4. Lightly butter a 25 x 30cm ovenproof dish.

Pour the milk, double cream and evaporated milk into a large saucepan. Using the point of a small, sharp knife, scrape out the seeds from the vanilla pods directly into the pan and add the pods too. Place over a medium-high heat until bubbles start to appear around the edge of the pan. Turn off the heat.

Using either a freestanding mixer fitted with the beater attachment or an electric hand mixer and large bowl, beat the 6 egg yolks and brown sugar together until creamy and fluffy. Add the flour and continue to mix until fully incorporated.

Remove the vanilla pods from the hot creamy milk then pour it onto the whisked mixture and whisk to combine. Strain through a sieve back into the pan and cook, stirring, over a low heat for a few minutes until the mixture thickens. Pour into a large, clean bowl and leave to cool completely.

Making sure the bowl and beaters are scrupulously clean, whisk the egg whites until they form soft peaks that just hold their shape. Add the caster sugar a spoonful at a time, whisking well after each addition until the mixture is thick, smooth and glossy, and forms stiff peaks.

Fold the sweetcorn, baking powder and salt into the cooled custard mixture. Using a large metal spoon, mix a third of the egg whites into the custard to loosen it, then gently fold in the rest, being careful not to knock out the air.

Pour the batter into the prepared dish and bake for 20 minutes. Lower the oven setting to 160°C/Fan 140°C/Gas 3 and bake for a further 20–25 minutes, until the pudding is puffed up, golden brown and set. Serve with golden or maple syrup, and vanilla ice cream, cream or crème fraîche, if you like.

DATE & NUT BREAD

This irresistible soft, sweet, sticky bread is filled with dates and crunchy nuts. It's very easy to make and extremely versatile. Try it with cheese, or even with ice cream; it is also excellent toasted. MAKES 1 LOAF

A knob of butter, for greasing
200g pitted dates, preferably Medjool, chopped (about 10–12 large dates)
90g shelled walnuts, chopped
1½ tsp bicarbonate of soda
225ml boiling water
2 eggs
200g caster sugar
½ tsp salt
220g strong white bread flour

Preheat the oven to 180°C/Fan 160°C/Gas 4. Grease a 1kg loaf tin with butter and line the base and sides with non-stick baking parchment.

Put the dates, walnuts, bicarbonate of soda and boiling water into a large bowl and mix together thoroughly. Leave to stand for 10 minutes, to allow the dates to plump up. They will give the bread a lovely, gooey texture and sweetness.

In another large bowl, whisk the eggs and sugar together until well combined. Add the salt and bread flour and mix well with a wooden spoon. Pour in the date and nut mixture and stir well to combine.

Pour the batter into the loaf tin and level the surface with the back of a spoon or a spatula. Bake for 50–60 minutes, until the loaf is golden brown and a skewer inserted into the centre comes out clean.

Leave the bread to cool in the tin for 5–10 minutes, then turn out onto a wire rack and remove the parchment. Leave to cool completely before serving.

BUTTERMILK SCONES

These wonderfully light scones are delicious served with jam and clotted cream for a West Country cream tea. For some, whether you come from Devon or Cornwall determines if you put the cream or jam on first. I'm not bothered – to me they're both lush! They are also really good split, toasted and buttered, or with some good Cheddar melted on top. MAKES 8

375g plain flour, sifted, plus extra for dusting
1 tsp baking powder
1 tsp bicarbonate of soda
1 tsp fine salt
75g lard, chilled and diced
75g butter, chilled and diced
2 tbsp caster sugar
225ml buttermilk

To serve
Raspberry or strawberry jam
Clotted cream

Preheat the oven to 200°C/Fan 180°C/Gas 6. Line a baking sheet with non-stick baking parchment.

Sift the flour, baking powder, bicarbonate of soda and salt into a large bowl. Add the lard and butter pieces and use your fingertips to gently rub them into the mixture until it resembles fine breadcrumbs.

Mix in the sugar, using a fork. Pour in the buttermilk and bring the mixture together using a fork or table knife, just until you have a soft dough. Work lightly and be careful not to overmix or the scones will be tough.

Turn the dough out onto a lightly floured surface and gently roll it out to a 2.5cm thickness. Use a plain or fluted 5–6cm cutter dipped in flour to cut out the scones. Keep the spaces between the scones minimal as you're cutting them out, and dust the cutter with flour each time. It's best not to re-roll the trimmings to make more scones as the off-cuts will be tough.

Place the scones on the baking sheet, spacing them out evenly. Bake for about 15 minutes, until golden brown and well risen. Transfer to a wire rack to cool a little.

Ideally, serve the scones while still warm, with lashings of jam and clotted cream, though they're fine at room temperature too. They are best served on the day they're made.

BLUEBERRY MUFFINS

I'm very fond of these simple, classic breakfast muffins, with their moist, tender crumb and the lovely burst of acidity from the fruit. They're great as they are, or you could top them with the coconut icing I use for my carrot cake (page 240). MAKES 12

150g butter, softened
150g caster sugar
3 eggs, lightly beaten
150ml whole milk
375g plain flour, sifted
1 tbsp baking powder
½ tsp salt
225g blueberries

Preheat the oven to 200°C/Fan 180°C/Gas 6. Line a 12-hole muffin tin with paper cases.

Using a freestanding mixer fitted with the beater attachment, or an electric hand mixer and bowl, cream together the butter and sugar until the mixture is light, pale and fluffy.

Gradually add the eggs, beating well after each addition. Then pour in the milk, a little at a time, mixing lightly as you add it to the batter.

Sift together the flour, baking powder and salt and gently fold into the batter, being careful not to overwork the mixture as it could make the muffins tough. It's fine if the batter seems a little lumpy. Use a large metal spoon to fold in the blueberries – try not to squish them!

Using a dessertspoon, drop even dollops of the muffin mixture into the paper cases, filling each one about two-thirds full. Bake for 18–20 minutes, until the muffins are lightly golden brown, springy to the touch and a skewer inserted into the centre comes out clean.

Let the muffins cool in the tin for a couple of minutes before transferring them to a wire rack to cool completely. They will keep stored in an airtight container for a couple of days, but they're best enjoyed right away.

POPCORN BARS

Remember those Rice Krispie cakes that used to appear at almost every birthday tea when you were a kid? Well this is my take on them, using popcorn to make a more substantial treat. You can finish them with a bitter chocolate topping, to make them even more grown up, if you like. MAKES 12–16

For the popcorn bars
50g butter, plus extra for greasing
75g golden syrup
200g marshmallows
A pinch of salt
120g plain popcorn

For the topping (optional)
200g dark chocolate (70% cocoa solids), broken into small pieces
150ml double cream
1 tbsp honey

Lightly grease a 25cm square cake tin with butter, then line with non-stick baking parchment, letting some parchment hang over the sides of the tin to make it easier to lift out the popcorn later. Butter the parchment. Do prepare the tin now – the marshmallow-y mixture stiffens up quickly once the popcorn goes in, so the tin needs to be ready.

Put the butter and golden syrup into a large saucepan and melt together over a low heat. Add the marshmallows and let them melt gently too, stirring. Add the salt and then fold in the popcorn, mixing well to make sure it's well coated.

Immediately pour the mixture into the prepared tin, spreading it to the corners with a spoon and pressing down gently to make a firm, even layer. Leave to cool and set.

For the topping, if making, melt the chocolate in a heatproof bowl over a pan of barely simmering water, making sure the bottom of the bowl is not touching the water. Meanwhile, heat the cream in a saucepan until bubbles start to appear around the edges of the pan. Give the melted chocolate a stir, then pour on the cream and gently mix together using a spatula. Add the honey and stir to combine.

Lift the popcorn out of the tin and peel off the parchment. If you've made the chocolate topping, drizzle it over the popcorn and leave to set for an hour.

Cut the popcorn into bars or squares, using a sharp knife. Eat immediately, or store in an airtight tin for up to a week.

RED CHILLI ROCKY ROAD

Chocolate and chilli is a super pairing. In this recipe, a single chilli adds subtle heat, which works well with the bitter dark chocolate, the sweetness of the dried fruits and the crunchy toasted nuts and seeds, while marshmallows lend a lovely chewiness.
MAKES 12–16 PIECES

A knob of butter, for greasing the tin
50g pecan nuts
250g dark chocolate (70% cocoa solids), broken into small pieces
50g shelled blanched pistachio nuts (bright green ones if you can find them)
50g dried mango, chopped
50g dried morello cherries
50g large marshmallows, chopped
2 tbsp pumpkin seeds
2 tbsp honey
1 tbsp olive oil
1 red chilli, deseeded and finely chopped
A pinch of salt

Preheat the oven to 180°C/Fan 160°C/Gas 4. Lightly grease a 20cm square cake tin with butter and line the base and sides with non-stick baking parchment.

Scatter the pecans in a single layer on a large baking tray and toast in the oven for about 5–7 minutes until fragrant and lightly coloured.

Put the chocolate into a large heatproof bowl and place over a pan of barely simmering water, making sure the bottom of the bowl is not touching the water. Once melted, give it a stir and remove from the heat. Leave to cool for a couple of minutes.

Using a spatula or large spoon, fold the rest of the ingredients into the melted chocolate. Mix together thoroughly, so that everything is well coated.

Pour the mixture into the lined tin, pressing it evenly into the corners with a spoon. Cover with cling film and refrigerate for at least 1–2 hours, until set.

Cut the rocky road into bars or squares, using a sharp knife. They will keep, sealed in a container in the fridge, for a couple of weeks.

CHOCOLATE NUT COOKIES

This is my failsafe chocolate chip recipe, the one I reach for more often than not. That little bit of salt works so well with the sweetness, enabling the rest of the flavours to shine. The trick with these cookies is not to overcook them, as they continue to firm up as they cool. MAKES 18–20

110g butter, softened
½ tsp fine salt
180g soft light brown sugar
170g plain flour, plus extra
   for dusting
2 tbsp whole milk
90g shelled hazelnuts,
   toasted and skinned (see
   page 24), then chopped
180g dark chocolate (70%
   cocoa solids), coarsely
   chopped

Using a freestanding mixer fitted with the paddle attachment, or an electric hand mixer and bowl, beat the butter and salt together. Add the brown sugar and flour and continue to mix to a rough paste, then stir in the milk. Finally add the chopped toasted hazelnuts and chocolate and mix briefly to combine.

Transfer the cookie dough to a lightly floured surface and divide in half. Using floured hands, roll each piece of dough into a thick log shape – how thick depends on how big you want your cookies, and how many you want to make!

Wrap the dough in cling film and refrigerate for at least an hour to firm up, or freeze for 30 minutes or so.

Preheat the oven to 170°C/Fan 150°C/Gas 3½. Line a couple of baking sheets with non-stick baking parchment.

Remove the cookie dough from the fridge and peel off the cling film. Using a sharp knife, cut the dough into roughly 1cm thick slices - it should be firm and easy to cut. Lay the slices on the prepared baking sheets, leaving space in between as they will spread slightly as they cook.

Bake for 8-11 minutes, until the cookies are lovely and golden brown, but still a little soft and chewy in the middle. Remove from the oven. At this point if you would like a neater edge to your cookies, while they're still warm, take a slightly smaller round cutter and cut the rough edges away.

Leave the cookies on the baking sheets for a couple of minutes, then transfer them to a wire rack to cool completely. They will keep in an airtight container for 3-4 days.

FUNNEL CAKES

These are called funnel cakes because they are formed by letting batter drop out of a funnel into hot oil, where they puff up into light little 'cakes', which are rather like doughnuts or Spanish churros in texture. Coated in cinnamon sugar, they are best eaten still warm. MAKES 15–20

Vegetable oil, for deep-frying
1 egg
160ml whole milk, plus
    a little extra if needed
175g plain flour
40g caster sugar
1 tsp baking powder
A pinch of salt

For the coating
3 tbsp icing sugar, sifted
1½–2 tsp ground cinnamon

Heat about a 15cm depth of oil in a deep-fat fryer to 180°C. Or use a large, deep pan, making sure it is no more than a third full, as the oil will bubble up ferociously as you add the batter. Use a frying thermometer to check the temperature, if you have one; otherwise drop a cube of dry white bread into the hot oil to test it – if the bread turns golden brown in just under a minute, the oil is up to temperature. Keep a close eye on it and never leave the pan unattended, even for a minute.

While the oil is heating, make the batter. Whisk the egg and milk together in a bowl until combined. In a separate bowl, whisk together the flour, sugar, baking powder and salt. Pour in the egg and milk mixture and whisk until smooth. Transfer the batter to a jug – to make it easier to pour into the funnel.

For the coating, mix the icing sugar and cinnamon together in a small bowl. Tip onto a plate and set aside.

You'll need to cook the funnel cakes a few at a time and bring the oil back up to temperature between batches. To proceed, pour the batter into a small funnel, keeping your finger over the nozzle to prevent it from pouring out. Very carefully, hold the funnel over the hot oil – its base should be at least 12cm above the oil, to be safe. Release your finger and let the batter drizzle into the fryer, gently swirling the funnel around in a snail-like pattern to create small spiral shapes. The batter should flow easily out of the funnel. If it's too thick, thin it with a little more milk before continuing.

Cook the funnel cakes for 1–2 minutes on each side, carefully turning them with a slotted spoon as necessary. Once they're golden brown and crisp, remove with the slotted spoon and drain on a tray or plate lined with kitchen paper. Immediately roll the funnel cakes in the cinnamon sugar, shaking off the excess, then serve straight away.

WHITE CHOCOLATE & PISTACHIO BLONDIES

These make a tempting, sophisticated alternative to the more familiar dark chocolate brownies. The earthy flavour of the sesame seeds and oil works so beautifully with white chocolate, balancing out its sweetness. Sprinkling on a little flaky sea salt at the end is a lovely finishing touch. MAKES 16

300g plain flour
2 tsp baking powder
A pinch of salt
100g shelled pistachio nuts, (bright green ones if you can find them), roughly chopped
200g white chocolate, roughly chopped
50g sesame seeds
150g butter, plus extra for greasing
300g demerara sugar
40ml rapeseed oil
40ml sesame oil
2 eggs, lightly beaten
1 vanilla pod, split in half lengthways
Flaky sea salt, to finish

Preheat the oven to 180°C/Fan 160°C/Gas 4. Lightly grease a 25cm square cake tin with butter and line the base and sides with non-stick baking parchment, letting some overhang the sides of the tin, to make it easier to lift out the cake later.

Put the flour, baking powder and salt into a large bowl and mix well, using a balloon whisk, to combine. Stir in the pistachios, 100g of the chocolate and the sesame seeds.

Melt the butter in a large saucepan over a very low heat, then add the demerara sugar, rapeseed and sesame oil, and the eggs. Using the point of a small, sharp knife, scrape out the seeds from the vanilla pod directly into the pan. Heat very gently for 3–4 minutes, whisking constantly, to combine and warm through – don't overheat or the eggs will curdle.

Pour the warm mixture onto the dry ingredients and whisk until thoroughly combined and the chocolate has melted. Finally, fold in the remaining chopped chocolate.

Pour the cake batter into the prepared cake tin and bake for 25–30 minutes, until cooked through. It should be lightly golden and quite firm to the touch. If a skewer inserted into the centre comes up slightly tacky that's fine, as it means the blondie will be nice and moist in the centre.

Remove from the oven and sprinkle on a generous pinch of flaky sea salt. Leave in the tin for 10 minutes, then lift out, peel away the parchment and place on a wire rack to cool.

Cut into squares to serve. The blondies will keep for 4–5 days in an airtight tin.

GOLDEN SYRUP GÂTEAU

This is one of my favourite cakes to enjoy with a cup of coffee. You can posh it up if you like and serve it with ice cream as a dessert, but for me, it's something I like as an afternoon treat. The frosted almonds finish it off nicely but you can serve the gâteau simply dusted with icing sugar if you prefer. MAKES 8 SLICES

115g butter, softened, plus
    extra for greasing
100g caster sugar
170g golden syrup
75ml boiling water
1 egg, plus 1 extra egg yolk
310g plain flour
1 tsp salt
1 tsp bicarbonate of soda
1 tsp baking powder
1 tsp freshly grated nutmeg
1 tsp ground cinnamon
½ tsp ground mace

For the icing
180g unsalted butter,
    softened
180g soft light brown sugar

For the frosted almonds
250g caster sugar
200g whole blanched
    almonds, lightly toasted
    (as for the pecans on
    page 230) and cooled

To finish (optional)
Sugar or icing sugar, to dust

Preheat the oven to 180°C/Fan 160°C/Gas 4. Lightly grease a 23cm springform cake tin with butter and line the base and sides with non-stick baking parchment.

Using a freestanding mixer fitted with the beater attachment, or an electric hand mixer and bowl, beat the butter and sugar together until the mixture is pale, light and fluffy. Add the golden syrup and beat for a minute or two. Mix in the boiling water, then add the egg and egg yolk and beat until smooth.

Sift together the flour, salt, bicarbonate of soda, baking powder, nutmeg, cinnamon and mace into a separate bowl. Add to the cake mixture, a little at a time, making sure each addition is fully incorporated before the next is added; try not to over-mix.

Pour the mixture into the prepared cake tin and bake for 30–35 minutes, until well risen, lightly golden and a skewer inserted into the centre comes out clean. Leave to cool in the tin for 10 minutes, then remove and carefully peel off the parchment. Place on a wire rack and leave to cool completely.

To make the icing, using a mixer, beat the butter and brown sugar together until the mixture is light, fluffy and smooth.

To prepare the frosted almonds, warm the caster sugar in a saucepan over a medium heat until it just starts to melt and colour. Add the toasted almonds and stir until the sugar has crystallised and coats the nuts. Tip onto a baking sheet and cool. Coarsely chop half the almonds; leave the rest whole.

Place the cake on a plate or cake stand. Using a palette knife, spread the icing all over the top, swirling it to create a lovely textured finish, and top with the frosted almonds. Finish with a dusting of sugar or icing sugar, if you like.

CARROT CAKE WITH COCONUT ICING

The combination of carrot and coconut is a fantastic one, especially when teamed with lots of spices and some lively orange zest. I love this cake with a cup of coffee, but it makes a delicious pudding too – serve a nice big slice with a scoop of coconut ice cream and you'll see what I mean. MAKES 8–10 SLICES

A little butter, for greasing
125ml rapeseed oil
120g soft light brown sugar
4 eggs
Finely grated zest and juice
    of 1 unwaxed orange
2 tbsp black treacle
1 vanilla pod, split in half
    lengthways and seeds
    scraped out
240g plain flour
2 tsp baking powder
2 tsp salt
2 tsp ground cinnamon
2 tsp freshly grated nutmeg
2 tsp ground mace
2 tsp cracked black pepper
240g carrots, coarsely grated
75g sultanas
75g walnuts, chopped

For the coconut icing
150g mascarpone
100g unsalted butter,
    softened
100g desiccated coconut
200g icing sugar

To finish
80g desiccated coconut,
    lightly toasted in a
    dry pan

Preheat the oven to 180°C/Fan 160°C/Gas 4. Lightly grease a 23cm springform cake tin with butter and line the base and sides with non-stick baking parchment.

Using a freestanding mixer fitted with a paddle attachment, or an electric hand mixer and large bowl, beat the oil, sugar, eggs, orange zest and juice, treacle and vanilla seeds together until fully combined.

Sift the flour, baking powder, salt, cinnamon, nutmeg and mace together over the mixture. Sprinkle over the black pepper, then scatter over the grated carrots, sultanas and chopped walnuts. Gently fold everything together with a spatula until evenly combined, but be careful not to overwork the mix. The batter should be fairly soft and a little runny.

Pour the mixture into the prepared cake tin and bake for about 40 minutes, until nicely golden and springy to the touch. To test, insert a skewer into the centre of the cake: it should come out clean. Leave to cool in the tin for 5–10 minutes, then turn out onto a wire rack and carefully remove the parchment. Leave the cake to cool completely.

To make the icing, using either a freestanding mixer with the paddle attachment or electric hand mixer and large bowl, beat the mascarpone and butter together until smooth. Beat in the coconut, then sift the icing sugar over the mixture and beat until the icing is smooth.

Using a palette knife, spread the icing all over the top and sides of the cake. To finish, sprinkle on the toasted coconut. Serve cut into generous slices.

FLOURLESS DARK CHOCOLATE CAKE

This is so simple, once you've made it, it will become your 'go to' chocolate cake every time you need a special treat. Cooked at a low temperature and left to set as it cools, it will then stay perfectly soft and moist in a tin for several days. MAKES 8–10 SLICES

250g butter, diced, plus extra
 for greasing
375g dark chocolate (70%
 cocoa solids), broken into
 small pieces
7 eggs, plus 1 extra egg yolk
375g caster sugar

To serve
Whipped cream or crème
 fraîche
Raspberries, toasted nuts
 and/or grated chocolate
 (optional)

Preheat the oven to 140°C/Fan 120°C/Gas 1. Lightly grease a 23cm springform cake tin with butter and line the base and sides with non-stick baking parchment.

Put the butter and chocolate into a large, heatproof bowl and place over a saucepan of barely simmering water, making sure the bottom of the bowl is not touching the water. Allow to melt, then stir until smooth. Remove the bowl from the heat and cool slightly.

Using a freestanding mixer fitted with the whisk, or an electric hand mixer and bowl, whisk the eggs, egg yolk and sugar together until the mixture is light, fluffy and increased in volume. Carefully pour in the melted mixture and fold gently with a spatula to combine, trying not to knock out any air.

Pour the cake mixture into the prepared tin. Bake for about 40–45 minutes until set. It will soufflé up a little and a crust will form on the top. Remove from the oven and leave to cool in the tin – the cake will settle and sink down in the centre.

Once it's cooled, press down and flatten the surface a little with a palette knife – this helps to give it a lovely, soft and gooey texture. Release the sides of the tin and peel away the parchment from the sides of the cake.

Invert a serving plate over the top of the cake and turn both over, to release the cake onto the plate. Remove the tin base and the baking parchment.

Either serve the cake just as it is, with cream or crème fraîche, or finish with any combination of whipped cream, raspberries, toasted nuts and grated chocolate.

BOOZY DATE AND BANANA MILK SHAKE

This is a proper grown-up milkshake. It's so easy and good – the earthy sweetness of the dates is great with the banana, and the splash of rum really perks everything up.
SERVES 2

250ml whole milk
200g pitted dates, preferably Medjool (about 10–12 large dates)
4 scoops of vanilla ice cream
1 ripe banana, broken into pieces
75ml rum
Finely grated zest of 1 unwaxed lime

These milk shakes are so easy! Simply whiz the milk, pitted dates, ice cream, banana, rum and lime zest together in a jug blender until smooth.

Depending on how you like the consistency, you can always add a splash of water or more milk to loosen.

Pour the milkshake into glasses and drink immediately – what could be simpler?

CONTINENTAL HOT CHOCOLATE

A long walk in the cold with my dogs, then home to sit in front of an open fire with a big bowl of this hot chocolate, is my idea of the perfect way to spend a winter afternoon. SERVES 4

2 tbsp cocoa powder
1 tbsp instant coffee
    granules
2 tsp cornflour
½ tsp ground mace
½ tsp salt
750ml whole milk
2 tbsp honey
125g dark chocolate (70%
    cocoa solids), broken into
    small pieces

To finish
1–2 tbsp extra virgin olive oil
Extra dark chocolate, grated

In a large bowl, stir together the cocoa powder, coffee granules, cornflour, mace and salt until evenly combined.

Pour the milk into a saucepan and place over a medium-low heat until almost simmering. When bubbles start to appear around the edges of the pan, pour the hot milk onto the cocoa mixture, whisking continuously to combine.

Return the mixture to the pan and place over a low heat. Simmer gently for 3–4 minutes, stirring continuously, until it has thickened. Stir in the honey and chocolate. Remove from the heat and whisk until the chocolate has melted and is fully incorporated.

Pour the hot chocolate into bowls or mugs. Finish with a trickle of olive oil and a sprinkling of grated chocolate, and enjoy immediately.

ACKNOWLEDGEMENTS

A few quick shout outs and thank yous. First off, to my superstar wife, Bef, for being so supportive. Love you, babe.

A big thank you to The Hand & Flowers and Coach crew for giving me the space, time and foundations for writing another book – love you all (apart from the person who still hasn't owned up to putting the tweezers in the toaster). An extra special thanks to the crew who came and played around with food for the book, making the recipes look great while singing along to top tunes on the radio: Aaron Mulliss, Nick Beardshaw, Jamie May, George O'Leary, Luke Henderson, Connor Black, Kane Williams, Josh Wilde, Sarah Hayward and Freddie Cook.

Now for the home economists and stylists – the people who grab the food and who make it all happen – Nicole Herft, Chris Mackett and Lydia Brun, as well as the fantastic team around them, including Jessica Mills, Victoria Bucknall, Emma Laws, Holly Cochrane and Catrine Håland. Thanks also to Jo McKenna. A big thank you to Richard Sinclair for the loan of his space for a couple of weeks; sorry we made such a mess!

You can never underestimate the importance of the typists – without them, there wouldn't be anything for you lot to read! They are the ever-amazing Alex Longstaff and (shhh!) LLH.

Thanks once again to the great Debora Robertson for taking the pain away; you make my life so easy. Love your work mate, shame about your football team though, ha ha!

A massive thanks to the team at Absolute and Bloomsbury: Jon Croft, Natalie Bellos, Xa Shaw Stewart, Alison Glossop, Ellen Williams and Marina Asenjo, as well as editor Janet Illsley and designer David Eldridge at Two Associates.

And a must-mention for the always impressive, truly stunning and brilliant Cristian Barnett, one of the most talented individuals I've ever come across. He is a man who showcases many skills, but above all, vision. And he is just an all-round lovely guy to talk to. Thanks also to Cristian's trusty sidekick, Brid. Without you two, I'd just have taken a load of rubbish shots on Instagram...

And lastly, a massive thank you to Borra and Louise at DML and Zoe at Samphire for all your great work and for trying your best to keep me out of trouble!

Big love,
Tom x

Absolute Press
An imprint of Bloomsbury Publishing Plc

50 Bedford Square
London
WC1B 3DP
UK

1385 Broadway
New York
NY 10018
USA

www.bloomsbury.com

First published in Great Britain 2015

British Library Cataloguing-in-Publication Data:
A catalogue record for this book is available from
the British Library.

Library of Congress Cataloguing-in-Publication
data has been applied for.

ISBN: HB: 978 1 4729 0943 5
       ePub: 978 1 4729 0944 2

2 4 6 8 10 9 7 5 3 1

Project editor: Janet Illsley
Designer: Two Associates
Photographer: Cristian Barnett, crisbarnett.com
Food styling: Tom Kerridge, Nicole Herft, Aaron
       Mulliss and Chris Mackett
Art direction and styling: Lydia Brun
Index: Hilary Bird

For ceramics and tiles, thanks to the following:
Akiko Hirai, akikohiraiceramics.com
Caroline Haurie, carolinehaurie.com
Dylan Bowen, dylanbowen.co.uk
Fired Earth, firedearth.com
Heather Gabriel, heathergabrielceramics.com
Helen Billingsley, helenbillingsleyceramics.co.uk
Krystyna Sargent, krystynasargent.com
Stine Dulong, skandihus.co.uk
Trudy Crane, lookslikewhite.com
Rebecca Williams, rebeccawilliams.uk

Printed and bound in Germany by Mohn Media.

To find out more about our authors and books
visit www.bloomsbury.com. Here you will
find extracts, author interviews, details of
forthcoming events and the option to sign up
for our newsletters.

*A note about the text: This book has been typeset
in Diaria, a seriffed, highly legible typeface that
was released in 2015.*

Innovative use of combined heat and power
technology when printing this product reduced
CO_2 emissions by up to 52% in comparison to
conventional methods in Germany.

MIX
Paper from
responsible sources
FSC® C011124